LANGUAGE!

The Comprehensive Literacy Curriculum

Jane Fell Greene, Ed.D.

SOPRIS WEST EDUCATIONAL SERVICES
A CAMBIUM LEARNING COMPANY

BOSTON, MA • NEW YORK, NY • LONGMONT, CO

08 07 06 05   10 9 8 7 6 5 4 3 2 1

Editorial Director: Nancy Chapel Eberhardt
Word and Phrase Selection: Judy Fell Woods
English Learners: Jennifer Wells Greene
Lesson Development: Sheryl Ferlito, Donna Lutz
Morphology: John Alexander, Mike Minsky, Bruce Rosow
Text Selection: Sara Buckerfield, Jim Cloonan
Decodable Text: Jenny Hamilton, Steve Harmon

LANGUAGE! eReader is a customized version of the CAST eReader for Windows® (version 3.0). CAST eReader © 1995–2003, CAST, Inc. and its licensors. All rights reserved.

ISBN 1-59318-264-3

Printed in the United States of America

Published and distributed by

SOPRIS
WEST
EDUCATIONAL SERVICES

4093 Specialty Place • Longmont, CO 80504 • (303) 651-2829
www.sopriswest.com

Table of Contents

Check off the activities you complete with each lesson. Evaluate your accomplishments at the end of each lesson. Pay attention to teacher evaluations and comments.

Unit Objectives	Lesson 1 (Date:_____)	Lesson 2 (Date:_____)
STEP 1 **Phonemic Awareness and Phonics** • Say the sounds for consonants <u>m</u>, <u>s</u>, <u>t</u>, <u>c</u>, <u>f</u>, and <u>b</u>. • Write the letters for sounds /m/, /s/, /t/, /k/, /f/, and /b/. • Distinguish the two sounds for <u>s</u>: /s/ and /z/. • Say the short sound for the vowel <u>a</u>. • Write the letter for the short vowel sound /a/.	❑ Move It and Mark It ❑ Phonemic Drills ❑ See and Say ❑ Exercise 1: Say and Write ❑ Exercise 2: Handwriting Pretest	❑ Move It and Mark It ❑ Consonant Chart (T) ❑ Phonemic Drills ❑ See and Say ❑ Say and Write
STEP 2 **Word Recognition and Spelling** • Read and spell words with sound-spelling correspondences from this unit. • Read and spell the **Essential Words**: *a, are, I, is, that, the, this*.	❑ Exercise 3: Spelling Pretest ❑ Build It ❑ Bank It ❑ Memorize It	❑ Build It, Bank It ❑ Word Fluency 1 ❑ Memorize It ❑ Exercise 1: Handwriting Practice
STEP 3 **Vocabulary and Morphology** • Define **Unit Vocabulary** words. • Add -s to mean more than one.	❑ Unit Vocabulary ❑ Multiple Meaning Map (T)	❑ Sort It (T)
STEP 4 **Grammar and Usage** • Identify nouns and verbs. • Identify words with multiple functions. • Build sentences with a noun/verb pattern.	❑ Introduction: Nouns ❑ Exercise 4: Find It	❑ Introduction: Verbs ❑ Exercise 2: Find It
STEP 5 **Listening and Reading** • Select the topic and details from informational text.	❑ Phrase Fluency 1 ❑ Exercise 5: Sentence Morphs	❑ Phrase Fluency 1 ❑ Exercise 3: Sentence Morphs ❑ Mini-Dialogs 1–4
STEP 6 **Speaking and Writing** • Generate sentences that present facts (statements). • Answer questions beginning with **is** and **are**. • Record information on a graphic organizer.	❑ Masterpiece Sentences: A Six-Stage Process ❑ Masterpiece Sentences: Stage 1	❑ Masterpiece Sentences: Stage 1 ❑ Write Your Own Mini-Dialog (T)
Self-Evaluation (5 is the highest) **Effort** = I produced my best work. **Participation** = I was actively involved in tasks. **Independence** = I worked on my own.	**Effort:** 1 2 3 4 5 **Participation:** 1 2 3 4 5 **Independence:** 1 2 3 4 5	**Effort:** 1 2 3 4 5 **Participation:** 1 2 3 4 5 **Independence:** 1 2 3 4 5
Teacher Evaluation	**Effort:** 1 2 3 4 5 **Participation:** 1 2 3 4 5 **Independence:** 1 2 3 4 5	**Effort:** 1 2 3 4 5 **Participation:** 1 2 3 4 5 **Independence:** 1 2 3 4 5

Lesson 3 (Date:_____)	Lesson 4 (Date:_____)	Lesson 5 (Date:_____)
☐ Move It and Mark It ☐ Vowel Chart (T) ☐ Phonemic Drills ☐ Exercise 1: Listening for Sounds in Words ☐ Letter-Sound Fluency	☐ Review: Vowels and Consonants ☐ Phonemic Drills ☐ Exercise 1: Listening for Sounds in Words ☐ Letter-Sound Fluency	☐ Phonemic Drills ☐ Letter-Sound Fluency ☐ Exercise 1: Say and Write ☐ Content Mastery: Learning the Code
☐ Exercise 2: Listening for Word Parts ☐ Word Fluency 1 ☐ Exercise 3: Find It	☐ Chain It (T) ☐ Word Fluency 2 ☐ Type It ☐ Exercise 2: Handwriting Practice	☐ Content Mastery: Spelling Posttest 1 ☐ Exercise 2: Sort It
☐ Define It (T)	☐ Just One: Singular Nouns ☐ Introduction: Plural Nouns ☐ Exercise 3: Singular Nouns and Plural Nouns ☐ English Plural—Sounds and Letters	☐ Exercise 3: Multiple Meanings
☐ Review: Nouns ☐ Exercise 4: Find It	☐ Nouns and Number ☐ Exercise 4: Just One or Two or More	☐ Exercise 4: Review: Noun or Verb
☐ Mini-Dialogs 5–8 ☐ Exercise 5: Instructional Text: "Batty About Bats!"	☐ Instructional Text: "Batty About Bats!" (T)	☐ Instructional Text: "Batty About Bats!" (T) ☐ Exercise 5: Which Wall?
☐ Answer It: Stage 1 ☐ Write Your Own Mini-Dialog (T)	☐ Blueprint for Writing (T) ☐ Challenge Text: "Bats in China"	☐ Exercise 6: Using the Blueprint for Writing ☐ Challenge Text: "Bats in China" ☐ Reading Response: "Bats in China"
Effort: 1 2 3 4 5 **Participation:** 1 2 3 4 5 **Independence:** 1 2 3 4 5	**Effort:** 1 2 3 4 5 **Participation:** 1 2 3 4 5 **Independence:** 1 2 3 4 5	**Effort:** 1 2 3 4 5 **Participation:** 1 2 3 4 5 **Independence:** 1 2 3 4 5
Effort: 1 2 3 4 5 **Participation:** 1 2 3 4 5 **Independence:** 1 2 3 4 5	**Effort:** 1 2 3 4 5 **Participation:** 1 2 3 4 5 **Independence:** 1 2 3 4 5	**Effort:** 1 2 3 4 5 **Participation:** 1 2 3 4 5 **Independence:** 1 2 3 4 5

Check off the activities you complete with each lesson. Evaluate your accomplishments at the end of each lesson. Pay attention to teacher evaluations and comments.

Unit Objectives	Lesson 6 (Date:_____)	Lesson 7 (Date:_____)
STEP 1 — **Phonemic Awareness and Phonics** • Say the sounds for consonants <u>m</u>, <u>s</u>, <u>t</u>, <u>c</u>, <u>f</u>, and <u>b</u>. • Write the letters for sounds / m /, / s /, / t /, / k /, / f /, and / b /. • Distinguish the two sounds for <u>s</u>: / s / and / z /. • Say the short sound for the vowel <u>a</u>. • Write the letter for the short vowel sound / a /.	❑ Review: Consonants and Vowels ❑ Move It and Mark It ❑ Phonemic Drills	❑ Move It and Mark It ❑ Phonemic Drills ❑ See and Say ❑ See and Name ❑ Exercise 1: Name and Write
STEP 2 — **Word Recognition and Spelling** • Read and spell words with sound-spelling correspondences from this unit. • Read and spell the **Essential Words**: a, are, I, is, that, the, this.	❑ Exercise 1: Spelling Pretest ❑ Build It, Bank It ❑ Word Fluency 3	❑ Build It, Bank It
STEP 3 — **Vocabulary and Morphology** • Define **Unit Vocabulary** words. • Add -s to mean more than one.	❑ Review: Vocabulary ❑ Exercise 2: Classify It	❑ Review: Two or More Plural Nouns ❑ Exercise 2: Sort It: Two or More ❑ Exercise 3: Phrase Dictation ❑ Exercise 4: Rewrite It
STEP 4 — **Grammar and Usage** • Identify nouns and verbs. • Identify words with multiple functions. • Build sentences with a noun/verb pattern.	❑ Introduction: Sentences ❑ Exercise 3: Diagram It 1	❑ Exercise 5: Sentence Review and Sentence Signals ❑ Exercise 6: Find It
STEP 5 — **Listening and Reading** • Select the topic and details from informational text.	❑ Phrase Fluency 2 ❑ Exercise 4: Sentence Morphs	❑ Phrase Fluency 2 ❑ Exercise 7: Sentence Morphs ❑ Mini-Dialogs 9–12
STEP 6 — **Speaking and Writing** • Generate sentences that present facts (statements). • Answer questions beginning with **is** and **are**. • Record information on a graphic organizer.	❑ Exercise 5: Masterpiece Sentences: Stage 1	❑ Masterpiece Sentences: Stage 1 ❑ Write Your Own Mini-Dialog (T)
Self-Evaluation (5 is the highest) **Effort** = I produced my best work. **Participation** = I was actively involved in tasks. **Independence** = I worked on my own.	**Effort:** 1 2 3 4 5 **Participation:** 1 2 3 4 5 **Independence:** 1 2 3 4 5	**Effort:** 1 2 3 4 5 **Participation:** 1 2 3 4 5 **Independence:** 1 2 3 4 5
Teacher Evaluation	**Effort:** 1 2 3 4 5 **Participation:** 1 2 3 4 5 **Independence:** 1 2 3 4 5	**Effort:** 1 2 3 4 5 **Participation:** 1 2 3 4 5 **Independence:** 1 2 3 4 5

Lesson 8 (Date:_____)	Lesson 9 (Date:_____)	Lesson 10 (Date:_____)
❑ Move It and Mark It ❑ Phonemic Drills ❑ Letter-Name Fluency	❑ Review: Vowel and Consonant Charts (T) ❑ Phonemic Drills ❑ Exercise 1: Listening for Sounds in Words ❑ Letter-Name Fluency	❑ Exercise 1: Listening for Sounds in Words
❑ Exercise 1: Sort It ❑ Exercise 2: Listening for Word Parts ❑ Word Fluency 4	❑ Exercise 2: Chain It	❑ Content Mastery: Spelling Posttest 2
❑ Content Mastery: Define It	❑ Multiple Meaning Map (T)	❑ Define It (T)
❑ Exercise 3: Sort It ❑ Exercise 4: Match It	❑ Exercise 3: Noun or Verb ❑ Mini-Dialogs (T)	❑ Content Mastery: Noun or Verb
❑ Mini-Dialogs 13–16 ❑ Exercise 5: Instructional Text: "Batty About Bats!"	❑ Instructional Text: "Batty About Bats!"	❑ Instructional Text: "Batty About Bats!" (T) ❑ Which Wall?
❑ Answer It ❑ Write Your Own Mini-Dialog (T)	❑ Blueprint for Writing (T) ❑ Challenge Text: "Casey at the Bat"	❑ Exercise 2: Blueprint for Writing (T) ❑ Challenge Text: "At Bat"
Effort: 1 2 3 4 5 **Participation:** 1 2 3 4 5 **Independence:** 1 2 3 4 5	**Effort:** 1 2 3 4 5 **Participation:** 1 2 3 4 5 **Independence:** 1 2 3 4 5	**Effort:** 1 2 3 4 5 **Participation:** 1 2 3 4 5 **Independence:** 1 2 3 4 5
Effort: 1 2 3 4 5 **Participation:** 1 2 3 4 5 **Independence:** 1 2 3 4 5	**Effort:** 1 2 3 4 5 **Participation:** 1 2 3 4 5 **Independence:** 1 2 3 4 5	**Effort:** 1 2 3 4 5 **Participation:** 1 2 3 4 5 **Independence:** 1 2 3 4 5

Exercise 1 · Say and Write

▶ Write the letter for each sound your teacher says.

▶ Say the sound as you write the letter.

1. _____   3. _____   5. _____   7. _____   9. _____

2. _____   4. _____   6. _____   8. _____   10. _____

Exercise 2 · Handwriting Pretest

_____

_____

_____

_____

_____

_____

Exercise 3 · Spelling Pretest

▶ Write the words your teacher says.

1. _____   6. _____

2. _____   7. _____

3. _____   8. _____

4. _____   9. _____

5. _____   10. _____

Exercise 4 · Find It: People, Places, and Things

▶ Listen and follow along as your teacher reads these paragraphs to you.

▶ Find the nouns—words that name people, places, and things.

▶ Underline the nouns.

---

based on "Batty About Bats!"

Bats fly. Bats have an extra skin. This skin connects their hands, arms, and ankles. Why do they have it? The skin forms wings. Bats use their wings to fly. They fly at night to find food. They need their wings to eat.

People sit and stand. Bats hang upside down, even when they sleep. Some bats live in trees. Some live in buildings. Others live in caves.

▶ Sort the nouns into the correct columns.

People	Places	Things

Exercise 5 · Sentence Morphs

▸ Practice scooping these phrases.

▸ Read as you would speak them.

the cat is fat The cat is fat.	Mac has the mat Mac has the mat.	Mac has the bats in the cab Mac has the bats in the cab.
the mats are in the cab The mats are in the cab.	I am at bat I am at bat.	I am Tam I am Tam.
Tam sat in the cab Tam sat in the cab.	Tam has a fat cat Tam has a fat cat.	Sam is at bat Sam is at bat.

Lesson 2

Exercise 1 · Handwriting Practice

_____

_____

_____

_____

_____

_____

_____

_____

Unit 1 · Lesson 2

Exercise 2 · Find It: Verbs

▶ Listen and follow along as your teacher reads these sentences to you.

▶ Find the **verb**—the word that answers:

> What did they (he, she, or it) do?

▶ Circle the verbs.

1. Bats fly.

2. Sam bats the ball.

3. Bats catch food at night.

4. People sit.

5. Bats hang in trees.

6. Some bats live in caves.

7. Cats stand.

8. Bats eat bugs.

9. Bats help crops.

10. The bats scatter seeds.

▶ Copy the words into the correct columns.

Can see the action	Can't see the action

Exercise 3 · Sentence Morphs

▸ Read the phrases.

▸ Scoop them.

the mats are in the cab The mats are in the cab.	Tam has a fat cat Tam has a fat cat.	Sam is at bat Sam is at bat.
the cat is fat The cat is fat.	I am at bat I am at bat.	I am Tam I am Tam.
Mac has the bats in the cab Mac has the bats in the cab.	Mac has the mat Mac has the mat.	Tam sat in the cab Tam sat in the cab.

Exercise 1 · Listening for Sounds in Words

▶ Put an X where you hear the short / *a* / sound.

1.

2.

3.

4.

5.

Exercise 2 · Listening for Word Parts

▶ Listen to each word.

▶ Write the part that your teacher repeats.

1. _____   6. _____

2. _____   7. _____

3. _____   8. _____

4. _____   9. _____

5. _____   10. _____

Exercise 3 · Find It: Essential Words

▸ Find the **Essential Words** in these sentences.

▸ Highlight or underline them.

1. Is this a mat?

2. That is the mast.

3. The cast acts.

4. This is a bat.

5. The cast is in this act.

6. The cabs are fast.

7. This is the cab.

8. I am in the fast cab.

9. Is that the cab?

10. I sat in the cab.

Write the **Essential Words** in the spaces.

_____   _____   _____

_____   _____

_____   _____

Unit 1 · Lesson 3

Exercise 4 · Find It: Nouns

▸ Listen and follow along as your teacher reads these sentences to you.

▸ Find the nouns—the people, places, and things.

▸ Underline the nouns.

> **based on "Batty About Bats!"**
>
> Bats help. Bats eat insects. Insects bite people and pets! Too many insects kill crops. Many farmers would lose their farms. People would not have food. Bats help get rid of insects.

▸ List each noun.

▸ Show if it belongs to people, places, or things with an X.

Nouns	People	Places	Things
bats			X

Exercise 5 · Instructional Text: "Batty About Bats!"

▸ Listen as your teacher reads to you.

▸ Underline the words with a short / *a* / as you hear them.

---

based on "Batty About Bats!"

Do mammals fly? One can fly. Which one? The bat can fly. Bats have an extra skin. It is thin. This skin connects parts of the bat. It joins its hands, arms, and ankles. The skin makes wings. Bats use the wings to fly. They fly at night. They look for food. They need their wings to eat.

Bats eat a lot. Flying takes energy. Food makes energy. Bats eat half their weight each day! They eat at night. Bats eat a lot of things. Some eat fruits. Some eat flowers. Some eat frogs and fish. Some eat lizards. Some eat bugs. They eat mosquitoes. They eat flies. They eat moths. They even eat termites!

---

1. What short / *a* / words did you hear? Write them here.

_____

_____

2. What are two things you know about bats?

_____

_____

3. What makes a bat a special mammal?

_____

_____

Exercise 1 · Listening for Sounds in Words

▶ The letter **s** can represent two sounds: / s / and / z /.

> **Examples: S Sounds**
>
> In **cats**, the **s** sounds like / s /.
>
> In **cabs**, the **s** sounds like / z /.

▶ Write the letters for the sounds in the words your teacher says.

▶ Circle the words in which the **s** sounds like / z /.

1.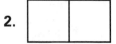

2.

3.

4.

5.

6.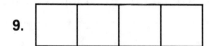

7.

8.

9.

10.

Exercise 2 · Handwriting Practice

▶ Copy these words: **a, I, the, this, that, is, are**

_____

_____

_____

_____

Exercise 3 · Singular Nouns and Plural Nouns

▶ **Just One: Singular Nouns**

> **Examples: Singular Nouns**
> The word **cat** means one cat.
> The word **mat** means one mat.
> The word **bat** means one bat.

▶ Listen as your teacher reads the sentences out loud.

▶ Fill in the blank.

The word **cab** means one _____ .

The word **scab** means one _____ .

The word **mast** means one _____ .

These are **singular** nouns.

(continued)

Unit 1 · Lesson 4

Exercise 3 (continued) · Singular Nouns and Plural Nouns

▸ **Two or More: Plural Nouns**

▸ Listen to the sentences.

▸ Underline words that end with **s**.

  1. Here are some facts about bats.

  2. Some bats eat bugs.

  3. Some bats eat fruits.

  4. They use wings to fly.

  5. Some bats live in dark caves.

The underlined words are **plural** nouns. **Plural** means two or more.
We use the letter **s** to make most nouns plural.

▸ Add **-s** and copy the plural nouns.

▸ Say the sound as you write each letter.

▸ Read out loud the plural nouns you have written.

Add -s	Copy the plural nouns
Example: mat ___s___	**Example:** ___mats___
1. bat _____	**1.** _____
2. cab _____	**2.** _____
3. cat _____	**3.** _____
4. tab _____	**4.** _____
5. fact _____	**5.** _____

▸ Use at least two of these plural nouns to say two complete sentences.

Exercise 4 · Just One or Two or More

▶ Listen and follow along as your teacher reads these sentences to you.

▶ Look at the underlined noun in each sentence.

▶ Circle "singular" or "plural" for the underlined noun.

	Just One	Two or More
1. Bats help.	singular	plural
2. Bats eat insects.	singular	plural
3. Insects bite people and pets.	singular	plural
4. Insects can kill a crop.	singular	plural
5. The farmer lost his farm.	singular	plural
6. Bats help get rid of insects.	singular	plural
7. Bats scatter seeds.	singular	plural
8. Bats hang upside down.	singular	plural
9. You might find bats in a cave.	singular	plural
10. Some hang in trees.	singular	plural

▶ Rewrite the sentences with singular nouns. Make the noun plural.

_____

_____

_____

Exercise 1 · Say and Write

▸ Write the letter for each sound your teacher says.

▸ Say the sound as you write the letter.

1. _____   3. _____   5. _____   7. _____   9. _____

2. _____   4. _____   6. _____   8. _____   10. _____

Exercise 2 · Sort It: Number of Sounds in Words

▸ Sort the words in the box below by the number of sounds you hear.

bat	cab	at	sat	ab
fat	cat	am	mat	tab

▸ Write the word in the correct column.

2 Sounds	3 Sounds

Exercise 3 · Multiple Meanings

▸ Listen and decide the correct meaning for **bat** in each sentence.

▸ Write the letter in the blank.

> **a.** animal
>
> **b.** sports equipment
>
> **c.** action

1. The baseball player **bats** at the ball. _____

2. The **bats** hung upside down in the cave. _____

3. The **bat** broke in two as the player hit the ball. _____

4. After he **bats,** the player runs the bases. _____

5. The **bat** helps by eating insects that kill crops. _____

6. The bear **bats** at the fish in the stream. _____

7. The baseball player picked up his **bat.** _____

8. The boy left his **bat** at home. _____

9. Farmers think that **bats** are helpful. _____

10. **Bats** see using sonar. _____

▸ Write a sentence using the word **bat.**

▸ Make sure the meaning of **bat** is clear.

_____

_____

_____

▸ Write the number of each sentence that uses **bat** as a verb. _____

Exercise 4 · Review: Noun or Verb

▶ Listen to your teacher read this information to you.

---

based on "Batty About Bats!"

Bats have wings. They have skin that connects parts of their bodies.
1   2

The skin makes wings. Bats use their wings to fly. They fly at night
3   4   5

to find food. Flying takes energy. Food makes energy. Bats eat a lot.
6   7   8

Some eat fruits and flowers. Some eat frogs, fish, and lizards. Some
9

eat flies and other bugs.
10

▶ Put an X to show if the word is a noun or verb.

▶ If it is a noun, put an X to show if it is singular or plural.

	The word is a		If it is a noun, it is	
	Noun	**Verb**	**Singular**	**Plural**
1. bats				
2. skin				
3. makes				
4. use				
5. fly				
6. food				
7. energy				
8. eat				
9. fruits				
10. flies				

Exercise 5 · Which Wall?

▸ Use the "Batty About Bats!" **Blueprint for Writing** graphic organizer to find the right "wall" for the answer.

▸ Write the "wall" in the blank.

1. Do mammals fly?

Wall: _____

2. What are bats' wings made of?

Wall: _____

3. What mammal flies at night?

Wall: _____

4. What else do bats do with their wings?

Wall: _____

5. What do bats eat?

Wall: _____

6. What kinds of bugs do bats eat?

Wall: _____

7. Do bats eat a lot?

Wall: _____

8. What flies at night?

Wall: _____

9. What do bats use to help them "see" at night?

Wall: _____

10. What do bats hear to help them "see"?

Wall: _____

Unit 1 · Lesson 5

Exercise 6 · Using the Blueprint for Writing

▸ Use the "Batty About Bats!" **Blueprint for Writing** graphic organizer and Exercise 5, **Which Wall?** for this exercise. Use the walls to help find the details to answer these questions.

1. What are bats' wings made of?

   _____

   _____

2. What else do bats do with their wings?

   _____

   _____

3. What do bats eat?

   _____

   _____

   _____

4. Do bats eat a lot?

   _____

   _____

5. What do bats use to help them "see" at night?

   _____

   _____

Lesson 6

Exercise 1 · Spelling Pretest

1. _____
2. _____
3. _____
4. _____
5. _____

6. _____
7. _____
8. _____
9. _____
10. _____

Exercise 2 · Classify It

▸ Use **Unit Vocabulary** (*Student Text,* page 4) and **Bank It** words.

▸ Find words that go together.

▸ Fill in the blanks.

1. _____ and _____ are both _____ .

2. _____ and _____ are both _____ .

3. _____ and _____ are both _____ .

4. _____ and _____ are both _____ .

5. _____ and _____ are both _____ .

Exercise 3 · Diagram It 1: Subject/Predicate

▸ Fill in the diagrams with your teacher.

▸ Use the diagrams to say a complete sentence.

1.

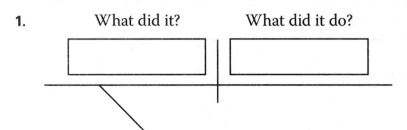

2.

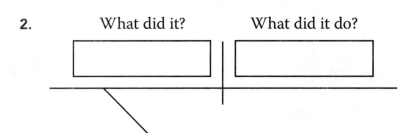

3.

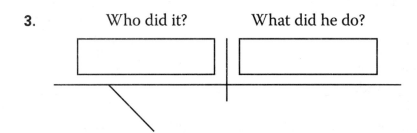

4.

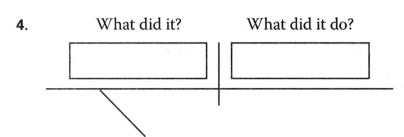

5.

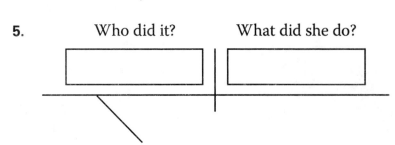

Exercise 4 · Sentence Morphs

▸ Practice scooping these sentences.

▸ Read as you would speak them.

this cat is fast This cat is fast.	Mac is a fast cat Mac is a fast cat.	Casey is at bat Casey is at bat.
the cast is in the cab The cast is in the cab.	I am in the cast I am in the cast.	Sam acts in the cast Sam acts in the cast.
Mac sat in the fast cab Mac sat in the fast cab.	that cab is fast That cab is fast.	the cast is in this act The cast is in this act.

Exercise 5 · Masterpiece Sentences: Stage 1

▸ Use the diagrams on page 26 to write **Stage 1** base sentences.

1. _____

2. _____

3. _____

4. _____

5. _____

Exercise 1 • Name and Write

▶ Write the letter for each sound your teacher says.

▶ Say the sound as you write the letter.

1. _____   3. _____   5. _____   7. _____   9. _____

2. _____   4. _____   6. _____   8. _____   10. _____

Exercise 2 • Sort It: Two or More

▶ Read each word.

1. cat	**5.** tabs	**9.** cats	**13.** masts	**17.** bat
2. cabs	**6.** cast	**10.** scab	**14.** mast	**18.** fats
3. mats	**7.** mat	**11.** acts	**15.** act	**19.** cab
4. tab	**8.** casts	**12.** scabs	**16.** facts	**20.** fast

▶ Sort the words in the columns below. Circle the plural nouns in which the final **s** sounds like / s /.

Just One	Two or More

Exercise 3 · Phrase Dictation

▶ Write the phrase your teacher says.

1. a fast cab
2. that act
3. that bad scab
4. the cats
5. mad bats
6. the mats
7. a cast

8. that bat
9. the mast
10. fast cabs
11. the fat bat
12. the masts
13. a cab
14. the fat bats

▶ Write the phrases in the correct column below.

Just One	Two or More

Exercise 4 · Rewrite It: Plural Nouns

▶ Read the sentence aloud.

▶ Change the underlined nouns from singular to plural.

▶ Rewrite the sentence with the plural noun.

▶ Read the new sentence aloud.

Just One	Two or More
1. We sat in the <u>cab</u>.	1. _____
2. The <u>cat</u> can bat the ball.	2. _____
3. The <u>bat</u> sat on the mast.	3. _____
4. The bats sat on the <u>mast</u>.	4. _____
5. The umpire has the <u>bat</u>.	5. _____

Exercise 5 · Sentence Review and Sentence Signals

▶ Read each sentence.

▶ Draw one line under the answer to show: Who (or what) did it?

▶ Draw two lines under the answer to show: What did they (he, she, or it) do?

▶ Circle the capital letter at the beginning of the sentence and the period at the end.

> **Example: Simple Sentence**
>
> The cat sat.

1. Mac bats the ball.

2. The cast sat in the cab.

3. Sam acts in the cast.

4. The umpire has the ball.

5. Casey has the bat.

Exercise 6 · Find It: Sentence Signals—Capitals and Periods

▶ Listen to your teacher read.

▶ Circle the capital letter at the beginning of the sentence and the period at the end.

---

from "Bats in China"

The Chinese decorated with bats. They embroidered bats on clothing. They painted bats on dishes. They carved bats. They displayed them in their homes. This brought happiness and long life. In their shrines, the Chinese used bats to honor their dead.

▶ How many sentences are there? _____

Exercise 7 · Sentence Morphs

▸ Read the phrases.

▸ Scoop them in the complete sentences.

• this cat • • is fast • This cat is fast.	• Casey • • is • • at bat • Casey is at bat.	• Sam • • acts • • in the cast • Sam acts in the cast.
• the cast • • is • • in the cab • The cast is in the cab.	• the cast • • is • • in this act • The cast is in this act.	• Mac • • is • • a fast cat • Mac is a fast cat.
• that cab • • is fast • That cab is fast.	• Mac • • sat • • in the fast cab • Mac sat in the fast cab.	• I • • am • • in the cast • I am in the cast.

Exercise 1 · Sort It: Consonant Combinations

▸ Sort the words in the box by the beginning and ending consonant combinations.

scab	mast	act	scat	stab
scam	cast	fact	fast	tact

▸ Write the words under the correct combinations.

sc-	st-	-st	-ct
_____	_____	_____	_____
_____	_____	_____	_____
_____	_____	_____	_____
_____	_____	_____	_____

Exercise 2 · Listening for Word Parts

▸ Listen to each word.

▸ Write the part that your teacher repeats.

1. _____	3. _____	5. _____	7. _____	9. _____
2. _____	4. _____	6. _____	8. _____	10. _____

Exercise 3 · Sort It: Subjects and Predicates

▸ Sort these phrases in the columns below.

a bat	a fast cab	this cat	sat in the cab
Sam	the cast	has a bat	acts in China
bats a ball	Casey	that cab	sat on the mat
the umpire	has a cast	Mac	has the ball

Who (or what) did it?	What did they (he, she, or it) do?

Unit 1 · Lesson 8

Exercise 4 · Match It

▸ Use the phrases from Exercise 3.

▸ Match a phrase from each column to make a sentence.

▸ Write it here.

▸ Check for sentence signals—capital letters and periods.

1. _____

2. _____

3. _____

4. _____

5. _____

Exercise 5 · Instructional Text

▸ Listen as your teacher reads to you.

---

from "Batty About Bats!"

Bats hang. They hang upside down. They hang when they sleep. Bats live in trees. Bats live in buildings. Bats live in caves. Many live in one cave. These are bat colonies.

Bats "go to bat" for the Earth. They eat a lot of bugs. Bats save plants. Bugs kill plants. Farmers can lose their farms. Millions would be hungry.

Bats help plants. They scatter seeds. Think about this. There is a fruit in Asia. It makes millions in cash. What if there were no bats? This plant could not grow. It could not spread. Farmers would lose the fruit. They would lose the cash.

---

1. What short / *a* / words did you hear? Write them here.

_____

2. What is a bat colony?

_____

3. How do bats help?

_____

Exercise 1 · Listening for Sounds in Words

▶ Put an X where you hear the sound.

1.
2.
3.
4.
5.
6.
7.
8.
9.
10.

Exercise 2 · Chain It

▸ Use your self-stick notes. Start with **cab.** Add or change the sound-spelling correspondence to make the next word your teacher says.

c a b

▸ Make a list of the words here:

_____

_____

_____

_____

_____

_____

_____

_____

_____

_____

Exercise 3 · Noun or Verb

▸ Look at **Mini-Dialogs 5, 6, 9, 10,** and **13–16**.

▸ Circle *noun* or *verb* for each word your teacher says.

1. noun or verb   5. noun or verb

2. noun or verb   6. noun or verb

3. noun or verb   7. noun or verb

4. noun or verb   8. noun or verb

Lesson 10

Exercise 1 · Listening for Sounds in Words

▶ Write the letters for the sounds you hear in each word.

▶ Circle the words your teacher tells you.

▶ Box the words your teacher tells you.

1.

2.

3.

4.

5.

6.

7.

8.

9.

10.

Exercise 2 · Which Wall?

▶ Use the "Batty About Bats!" **Blueprint for Writing** graphic organizer to find the right "wall" for the answer.

▶ Write the "wall" in the blank.

1. What are two things that people do to harm bats?

Wall: _____

Answer: _____

_____

2. What else do people do to harm bats?

Wall: _____

Answer: _____

_____

3. Where do bats live?

Wall: _____

Answer: _____

_____

4. Do bats live alone?

Wall: _____

Answer: _____

_____

5. What do bats do to help people?

Wall: _____

Answer: _____

_____

Check off the activities you complete with each lesson. Evaluate your accomplishments at the end of each lesson. Pay attention to teacher evaluations and comments.

Unit Objectives	Lesson 1 (Date:_____)	Lesson 2 (Date:_____)
STEP 1 **Phonemic Awareness and Phonics** • Say the sounds for consonants <u>n</u>, <u>l</u>, <u>h</u>, <u>r</u>, <u>j</u>, and <u>p</u>. • Write the letters for the sounds / n /, / l /, / h /, / r /, / j /, and / p /.	❑ Move It and Mark It ❑ Phonemic Drills ❑ See and Say ❑ Exercise 1: Say and Write ❑ Exercise 2: Handwriting Practice	❑ Move It and Mark It ❑ Consonant Chart ❑ Phonemic Drills ❑ See and Say ❑ Say and Write
STEP 2 **Word Recognition and Spelling** • Read and spell words with sound-spelling correspondences from this and the previous unit. • Read and spell the **Essential Words**: *do, said, to, who, you, your.*	❑ Exercise 3: Spelling Pretest ❑ Build It, Bank It ❑ Memorize It	❑ Build It, Bank It ❑ Word Fluency 1 ❑ Memorize It ❑ Exercise 1: Handwriting Practice
STEP 3 **Vocabulary and Morphology** • Define **Unit Vocabulary** words. • Identify and generate antonyms for **Unit Vocabulary**. • Add 's to mean singular possession.	❑ Unit Vocabulary ❑ Multiple Meaning Map (T)	❑ Unit Vocabulary ❑ Exercise 2: Sort It
STEP 4 **Grammar and Usage** • Identify the subject in a sentence. • Identify the predicate in a sentence. • Build simple sentences with one subject and one predicate.	❑ Review: Nouns and Verbs ❑ Exercise 4: Find It	❑ Introduction: Subject ❑ Exercise 3: Find It
STEP 5 **Listening and Reading** • Select the topic and details from informational text.	❑ Phrase Fluency 1 ❑ Exercise 5: Sentence Morphs	❑ Phrase Fluency 1 ❑ Exercise 4: Sentence Morphs ❑ Mini-Dialogs 1–4
STEP 6 **Speaking and Writing** • Generate sentences that present facts (statements). • Answer questions beginning with **who**. • Record information on a graphic organizer.	❑ Masterpiece Sentences: Stage 1	❑ Masterpiece Sentences: Stage 1 ❑ Write Your Own Mini-Dialog (T)
Self-Evaluation (5 is the highest) **Effort** = I produced my best work. **Participation** = I was actively involved in tasks. **Independence** = I worked on my own.	**Effort:** 1 2 3 4 5 **Participation:** 1 2 3 4 5 **Independence:** 1 2 3 4 5	**Effort:** 1 2 3 4 5 **Participation:** 1 2 3 4 5 **Independence:** 1 2 3 4 5
Teacher Evaluation	**Effort:** 1 2 3 4 5 **Participation:** 1 2 3 4 5 **Independence:** 1 2 3 4 5	**Effort:** 1 2 3 4 5 **Participation:** 1 2 3 4 5 **Independence:** 1 2 3 4 5

Lesson 3 (Date:_____)	Lesson 4 (Date:_____)	Lesson 5 (Date:_____)
❑ Move It and Mark It ❑ Vowel Chart (T) ❑ Phonemic Drills ❑ Exercise 1: Listening for Sounds in Words ❑ Letter-Sound Fluency	❑ Review: Vowels and Consonants ❑ Phonemic Drills ❑ Exercise 1: Listening for Sounds in Words ❑ Letter-Sound Fluency	❑ Phonemic Drills ❑ Letter-Sound Fluency ❑ Exercise 1: Say and Write ❑ Content Mastery: Learning the Code
❑ Exercise 2: Listening for Word Parts ❑ Word Fluency 1 ❑ Exercise 3: Find It	❑ Chain It (T) ❑ Word Fluency 2 ❑ Type It ❑ Exercise 2: Handwriting Practice	❑ Content Mastery: Spelling Posttest 1 ❑ Exercise 2: Sort It
❑ Unit Vocabulary ❑ Define It (T)	❑ Introduction: The Owner: Singular Possessive Nouns ❑ Exercise 3: The Owner: Singular Possessive Nouns ❑ Exercise 4: Find It	❑ Multiple Meaning Map (T)
❑ Introduction: Predicate ❑ Exercise 4: Find It	❑ Nouns: Singular Possessive ❑ Singular Possessive and Plural Nouns ❑ Exercise 5: Sort It	❑ Review: Subject or Predicate ❑ Exercise 3: Choose It: Subject or Predicate
❑ Mini-Dialogs 5–8 ❑ Exercise 5: Instructional Text: "A Map Is a Sandwich"	❑ Exercise 6: Instructional Text: "A Map Is a Sandwich"	❑ Instructional Text: "A Map Is a Sandwich" (T)
❑ Instructional Text: "A Map Is a Sandwich" ❑ Write Your Own Mini-Dialog (T)	❑ Blueprint for Writing (T) ❑ Challenge Text: "Mapping the Unknown"	❑ Exercise 4: Using the Blueprint for Writing ❑ Reading Response: "A Map Is a Sandwich" ❑ Challenge Text: "Mapping the Unknown"
Effort: 1 2 3 4 5 **Participation:** 1 2 3 4 5 **Independence:** 1 2 3 4 5	**Effort:** 1 2 3 4 5 **Participation:** 1 2 3 4 5 **Independence:** 1 2 3 4 5	**Effort:** 1 2 3 4 5 **Participation:** 1 2 3 4 5 **Independence:** 1 2 3 4 5
Effort: 1 2 3 4 5 **Participation:** 1 2 3 4 5 **Independence:** 1 2 3 4 5	**Effort:** 1 2 3 4 5 **Participation:** 1 2 3 4 5 **Independence:** 1 2 3 4 5	**Effort:** 1 2 3 4 5 **Participation:** 1 2 3 4 5 **Independence:** 1 2 3 4 5

Check off the activities you complete with each lesson. Evaluate your accomplishments at the end of each lesson. Pay attention to teacher evaluations and comments.

Unit Objectives	Lesson 6 (Date:_____)	Lesson 7 (Date:_____)
STEP 1 **Phonemic Awareness and Phonics** • Say the sounds for consonants n, l, h, r, j, and p. • Write the letters for the sounds / n /, / l /, / h /, / r /, / j /, and / p /.	❑ Review: Consonants and Vowels ❑ Introduction: Consonant Pairs ❑ Move It and Mark It ❑ Phonemic Drills ❑ See and Say ❑ Exercise 1: Handwriting Practice	❑ Move It and Mark It ❑ Phonemic Drills ❑ See and Say ❑ See and Name ❑ Exercise 1: Name and Write
STEP 2 **Word Recognition and Spelling** • Read and spell words with sound-spelling correspondences from this and the previous unit. • Read and spell the **Essential Words**: do, said, to, who, you, your.	❑ Exercise 2: Spelling Pretest ❑ Build It, Bank It ❑ Word Fluency 3 ❑ Handwriting Practice	❑ Build It, Bank It
STEP 3 **Vocabulary and Morphology** • Define **Unit Vocabulary** words. • Identify and generate antonyms for **Unit Vocabulary**. • Add 's to mean singular possession.	❑ Review: Vocabulary ❑ Exercise 3: Classify It	❑ Review: Singular Possessive Nouns and Plural Nouns ❑ Exercise 2: Sort It ❑ Exercise 3: Choose It and Use It ❑ Exercise 4: Find It
STEP 4 **Grammar and Usage** • Identify the subject in a sentence. • Identify the predicate in a sentence. • Build simple sentences with one subject and one predicate.	❑ Introduction: Simple Sentences ❑ Exercise 4: Diagram It	❑ Exercise 5: Sentence Dictation
STEP 5 **Listening and Reading** • Select the topic and details from informational text.	❑ Phrase Fluency 2 ❑ Exercise 5: Sentence Morphs	❑ Phrase Fluency 2 ❑ Exercise 6: Sentence Morphs ❑ Mini-Dialogs 9–12
STEP 6 **Speaking and Writing** • Generate sentences that present facts (statements). • Answer questions beginning with **who**. • Record information on a graphic organizer.	❑ Exercise 6: Masterpiece Sentences: Stage 1	❑ Masterpiece Sentences: Stage 1 ❑ Write Your Own Mini-Dialog (T)
Self-Evaluation (5 is the highest) **Effort** = I produced my best work. **Participation** = I was actively involved in tasks. **Independence** = I worked on my own.	**Effort:** 1 2 3 4 5 **Participation:** 1 2 3 4 5 **Independence:** 1 2 3 4 5	**Effort:** 1 2 3 4 5 **Participation:** 1 2 3 4 5 **Independence:** 1 2 3 4 5
Teacher Evaluation	**Effort:** 1 2 3 4 5 **Participation:** 1 2 3 4 5 **Independence:** 1 2 3 4 5	**Effort:** 1 2 3 4 5 **Participation:** 1 2 3 4 5 **Independence:** 1 2 3 4 5

Lesson 8 (Date:_____)	**Lesson 9** (Date:_____)	**Lesson 10** (Date:_____)
❑ Move It and Mark It ❑ Phonemic Drills ❑ Letter-Name Fluency ❑ Exercise 1: Sort It	❑ Review: Vowel and Consonant Charts (T) ❑ Phonemic Drills ❑ Exercise 1: Listening for Sounds in Words ❑ Letter-Name Fluency	❑ Exercise 1: Listening for Sounds in Words
❑ Exercise 2: Listening for Word Parts ❑ Word Fluency 4	❑ Exercise 2: Chain It	❑ Content Mastery: Spelling Posttest 2
❑ Exercise 3: Introduction: Antonyms ❑ Content Mastery: Define It	❑ Multiple Meaning Map (T)	❑ Define It (T)
❑ Exercise 4: Diagram It	❑ Exercise 3: Diagram It	❑ Content Mastery: Subject or Predicate
❑ Mini-Dialogs 13–16 ❑ Exercise 5: Instructional Text: "The Hardest Maps to Make"	❑ Instructional Text: "The Hardest Maps to Make"	❑ Instructional Text: "The Hardest Maps to Make" (T) ❑ Exercise 2: Which Wall?
❑ Instructional Text: "The Hardest Maps to Make" ❑ Write Your Own Mini-Dialog (T)	❑ Blueprint for Writing (T) ❑ Challenge Text: "Atlas: A Book of Maps"	❑ Exercise 3: Using the Blueprint for Writing ❑ Challenge Text: "Floki: Sailor Without a Map" ❑ Exercise 4: Map It
Effort: 1 2 3 4 5 **Participation:** 1 2 3 4 5 **Independence:** 1 2 3 4 5	**Effort:** 1 2 3 4 5 **Participation:** 1 2 3 4 5 **Independence:** 1 2 3 4 5	**Effort:** 1 2 3 4 5 **Participation:** 1 2 3 4 5 **Independence:** 1 2 3 4 5
Effort: 1 2 3 4 5 **Participation:** 1 2 3 4 5 **Independence:** 1 2 3 4 5	**Effort:** 1 2 3 4 5 **Participation:** 1 2 3 4 5 **Independence:** 1 2 3 4 5	**Effort:** 1 2 3 4 5 **Participation:** 1 2 3 4 5 **Independence:** 1 2 3 4 5

Exercise 1 · Say and Write

▸ Write the letter for each sound your teacher says.

▸ Say the sound as you write the letter.

1. _____   3. _____   5. _____   7. _____   9. _____

2. _____   4. _____   6. _____   8. _____   10. _____

Exercise 2 · Handwriting Practice

_____

_____

_____

_____

_____

_____

_____

_____

_____

Exercise 3 · Spelling Pretest

1. _____   6. _____

2. _____   7. _____

3. _____   8. _____

4. _____   9. _____

5. _____   10. _____

Exercise 4 · Find It: Noun or Verb

▸ Read the phrase.

▸ Decide if the **bold** word is a noun or a verb.

▸ Circle your choice.

1. **map** a plan	Noun	Verb
2. plan a **map**	Noun	Verb
3. an **act**	Noun	Verb
4. to **act** in	Noun	Verb
5. **jam** it in	Noun	Verb
6. canned the **jam**	Noun	Verb
7. the fast **ram**	Noun	Verb
8. to **ram** into	Noun	Verb
9. the baseball **fans**	Noun	Verb
10. to **fan** a man	Noun	Verb

Exercise 5 · Sentence Morphs

▶ Practice scooping these sentences.

▶ Read as you would speak them.

• the map • • is flat • The map is flat.	• who • • has the map • Who has the map?	• the mapmaker • • has the map • The mapmaker has the map.
• the cans • • are • • in the lab • The cans are in the lab.	• you • • said • • to ban labs • You said to ban labs.	• that • • is • • a tan cab • That is a tan cab.
• the man • • ran • • to the lab • The man ran to the lab.	• Al said • • is that Dad's cap • Al said, "Is that Dad's cap?"	• Nan • • has to plan • • a map • Nan has to plan a map.

Exercise 1 · Handwriting Practice

_____

_____

_____

_____

_____

_____

_____

Exercise 2 · Sort It: Meaning Categories

▶ Sort these words into categories. Some words are used more than once.

plant	map	man	you	plan
can	ran	pant	jam	mat
stamp	cat	raft	I	

Living things	Actions	Things that are flat

Unit 2 · Lesson 2

Exercise 3 · Find It: Subjects

▸ Listen and follow along as your teacher reads these sentences to you.

▸ Find the noun that is the subject—the word that answers:

> Who or what did it?

▸ Circle the noun that is the **subject.**

1. Mapmakers put marks on maps.

2. Early mapmakers decorated maps with creatures.

3. Maps show towns and rivers.

4. A map uses lines for roads.

5. People use maps on trips.

6. Some travelers get lost without maps.

7. Students draw maps in school.

8. Explorers needed maps.

9. Sailors used the sun and stars to find Asia.

10. The continents appear on big maps.

▸ Sort the nouns.

People	Places	Things

Exercise 4 · Sentence Morphs

▸ Practice scooping these sentences.

▸ Read as you would speak them.

the map is flat The map is flat.	the cans are in the lab The cans are in the lab.	the mapmaker has the map The mapmaker has the map.
Al said is that Dad's cap Al said, "Is that Dad's cap?"	you said to ban labs You said to ban labs.	who has the map Who has the map?
the man ran to the lab The man ran to the lab.	that is a tan cab That is a tan cab.	Nan has to plan a map Nan has to plan a map.

Exercise 1 · Listening for Sounds in Words

▸ Put an X where you hear the short / *a* / sound.

1.

2.

3.

4.

5.

Exercise 2 · Listening for Word Parts

▸ Listen to each word.

▸ Write the part that your teacher repeats.

1. _____   6. _____

2. _____   7. _____

3. _____   8. _____

4. _____   9. _____

5. _____   10. _____

Exercise 3 · Find It: Essential Words

▶ Find the **Essential Words** in these sentences.

▶ Underline them. (There may be more than one in a sentence.)

1. The man ran to the cab.

2. Pat ran to the lab.

3. Who can you tap?

4. You can map lines.

5. Is that your cap?

6. That is your fan.

7. Who is the man?

8. Who has the plans?

9. Diana can do that.

10. I can do the map.

11. Who said that?

12. You said that.

▶ Write the **Essential Words** in the spaces.

_____   _____   _____

_____   _____   _____

Unit 2 · Lesson 3

Exercise 4 · Find It: Predicates

▸ Listen and follow along as your teacher reads these sentences to you.

▸ Find the predicate—the words that answer:

> What did they (he, she, or it) do?

▸ Underline the **predicate**.

▸ Circle the **verb** in the **predicate**.

1. Mapmakers put marks on maps.

2. Early mapmakers decorated maps with creatures.

3. Maps show towns and rivers.

4. A map uses lines for roads.

5. People use maps on trips.

6. Many travelers find places with maps.

7. Students draw maps in school.

8. Explorers needed maps.

9. Sailors used the sun and stars to find Asia.

10. The continents appear on big maps.

Exercise 5 · Instructional Text: "A Map Is a Sandwich"

▸ Listen as your teacher reads to you.

---

from "A Map Is a Sandwich"

Making a map is like making a sandwich. Think about it. A sandwich has layers. First, there is a layer of bread. Then, there is a layer of mustard. Add lettuce. Next, add meat. Then add a layer of cheese. Last, add more bread.

Stacy and Diana are cartographers. They make maps. They need facts. They use facts from the sky. They get facts from land. Facts come from satellites. Facts come from surveys. Pictures of lines come to them. Diana and Stacy turn the lines into maps.

---

1. What short / *a* / words did you hear? Write them here.

   _____

   _____

2. What is a cartographer?

   _____

▸ Use the text to fill in the blanks.

Cartographers need _____ to make maps.

They get facts from _____ .

Facts from satellites and surveys help make _____ .

Exercise 1 · Listening for Sounds in Words

The letter **s** can represent two sounds: / s / and / z /.

> **Examples:**
>
> In **cats**, the **s** sounds like / s /.
>
> In **cabs**, the **s** sounds like / z /.

▸ Write the letters for the sounds in the words your teacher says.

▸ Circle the words in which the **s** sounds like / z /.

1.
2.
3.
4.
5.

6.
7.
8.
9.
10.

Exercise 2 · Handwriting Practice

▶ Copy these words: **to, you, who, do, said, your**

_____

_____

_____

_____

_____

_____

_____

_____

Exercise 3 · The Owner: Singular Possessive Nouns

▶ Listen to your teacher read each sentence out loud.

▶ Fill in the blanks.

1. The **man's map** means the _____ that belongs to the _____ .

2. **Ann's pan** means a _____ owned by _____ .

3. The **cab's red mat** means one _____ that belongs in the _____ .

4. **Sam's plant** means a _____ that belongs to _____ .

(continued)

Unit 2 · Lesson 4

Exercise 3 (continued) · The Owner: Singular Possessive Nouns

▶ These are **singular possessive nouns:** man's, Ann's, cab's, Sam's. The noun that shows ownership is singular.

▶ Add 's and copy the singular possessive noun and the phrase.

▶ Say the sound as you write each letter.

▶ Read the phrases out loud.

Add -s	Copy the phrase
Example: Sam**'s** map.	**Example:** Sam's map
1. Ann_____ raft	1. _____
2. Stan_____ cab	2. _____
3. Hal_____ raft	3. _____
4. the tramp_____ cabin	4. _____
5. the cat_____ nap	5. _____
6. Sal_____ pal	6. _____
7. the man_____ scam	7. _____
8. the mapmaker_____ plans	8. _____
9. Pat_____ bats	9. _____
10. Sam_____ clams	10. _____

Exercise 4 · Find It: Singular Possessive Nouns

▶ Listen to these sentences as your teacher reads.

▶ Underline the words that signal ownership.

▶ Draw an arrow to show what is owned.

1. Stan's town is on the map.

2. Ann's raft is on a river in Stan's town.

3. The mapmaker's map is a draft with black dots for towns.

4. Stan's camp and Ann's cabin are on Stacy's map.

5. We show Stacy's map to Pat and Dan.

6. The mapmakers scan Stacy's map for Stan's camp.

7. Pat and Dan blast to Stan's camp on Ann's raft.

8. Stan has Dan's tent and Pat's lamp at the camp.

9. Stan, Pat, and Dan had crabs and clams at Stan's camp.

Unit 2 · Lesson 4

Exercise 5 · Sort It: Singular Possessive or Plural Nouns

▸ Read these words.

1. cat's	**5.** clam's	**9.** tramps	**13.** mat's	**17.** Nan's
2. mats	**6.** rat's	**10.** masts	**14.** mast's	**18.** clams
3. cats	**7.** scabs	**11.** Ann's	**15.** cabs	**19.** Sam's
4. cast's	**8.** tramp's	**12.** Stan's	**16.** scraps	**20.** scab's

▸ Sort and copy them in the correct column.

▸ Say the sound as you write each letter and say "apostrophe" as you write each apostrophe.

The Owner— Singular Possessive	Two or More—Plural

Exercise 6 · Instructional Text: "A Map Is a Sandwich"

▸ Listen to the selection as your teacher reads.

▸ Think about the layers of the map.

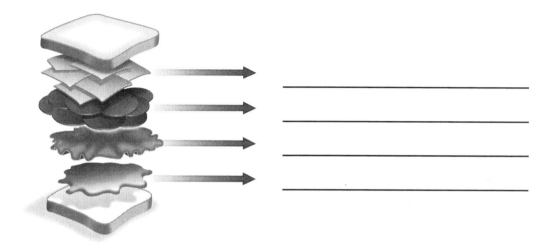

Exercise 1 · Say and Write

▶ Write the letter for each sound your teacher says.

▶ Say the sound as you write the letter.

1. _____   3. _____   5. _____   7. _____   9. _____

2. _____   4. _____   6. _____   8. _____   10. _____

Exercise 2 · Sort It: Number of Sounds

▶ Sort the words in the box by the number of sounds you hear.

can	cap	rat	as	an
lab	jam	tan	hat	nap

▶ Write each word in the correct number column.

Two sounds	Three sounds

Exercise 3 · Choose It: Subject or Predicate

▶ Listen to your teacher read this information to you.

---

based on "A Map Is a Sandwich"

Stacy and Diana <u>make maps</u>. They need facts. They <u>use facts from</u>
              1   2
<u>the sky</u>. <u>Satellites in the sky</u> provide facts about the land. More facts
              3
<u>come from surveys</u>. <u>Pictures of lines</u> come to Diana and Stacy. They
        4   5
<u>turn these lines into maps</u>. <u>Maps</u> use lines to show where there are
              6   7
rivers and roads. Stacy and Diana <u>decide the kinds of lines for the</u>
                                              8
<u>map</u>. Some lines <u>form borders</u>. Other lines represent roads. <u>Different</u>
                        9   10
<u>lines</u> are rivers. Each line means something.

▶ Write an X to show if the underlined words are subjects or predicates.

▶ If they are predicates, then write the verbs.

	Are the words		If they are predicates, then write the verbs.
	Subjects?	Predicates?	
1. make maps			
2. use facts from the sky			
3. satellites in the sky			
4. come from surveys			
5. pictures of lines			
6. turn these lines into maps			
7. maps			
8. decide the kinds of lines for the map			
9. form borders			
10. different lines			

Unit 2 · Lesson 5

Exercise 4 · Using the Blueprint for Writing

▸ Use **"A Map Is a Sandwich" Blueprint for Writing** graphic organizers to answer these questions.

1. What does a cartographer use to make maps?

_____

_____

2. What do the lines represent on a map?

_____

_____

3. What is color used for on a map?

_____

_____

4. What shows symbols on a map?

_____

_____

5. What does a map key use to give information?

_____

_____

Exercise 1 · Handwriting Practice

▶ Copy the Unit 2 **Essential Words**.

▶ Use correct letter formation.

to	you	your	who	do	said
___	___	___	___	___	___
___	___	___	___	___	___
___	___	___	___	___	___

Exercise 2 · Spelling Pretest

▶ Write the words your teacher says.

1. _____   6. _____

2. _____   7. _____

3. _____   8. _____

4. _____   9. _____

5. _____   10. _____

Unit 2 · Lesson 6

Exercise 3 · Classify It

▸ Use **Unit Vocabulary** (*Student Text,* page 38) and **Bank It** words.

▸ Find words that go together.

▸ Fill in the blanks.

1. _____ and _____ are both _____ .

2. _____ and _____ are both _____ .

3. _____ and _____ are both _____ .

4. _____ and _____ are both _____ .

5. _____ and _____ are both _____ .

Exercise 4 · Diagram It: Subject/Predicate

▸ Fill in the diagrams with your teacher.

▸ Use the diagrams to say a complete sentence.

1. What did it?   What did it do?

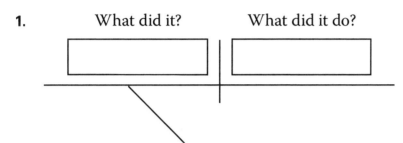

2. Who did it?   What did he do?

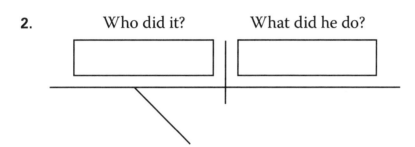

3. What did it?   What did it do?

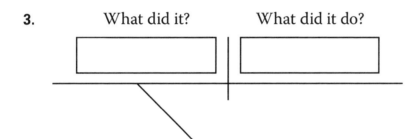

4. What did it?   What did it do?

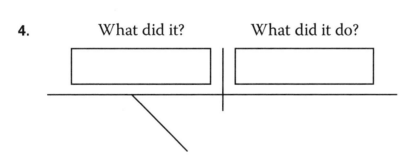

5. What did it?   What did it do?

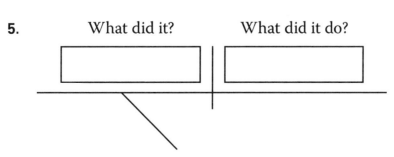

Exercise 5 · Sentence Morphs

▶ Practice scooping these phrases.

▶ Read as you would speak them.

• the plan • • is a trap • The plan is a trap.	• the scientist • • scans the plans • The scientist scans the plans.	• the mapmaker • • has the camp plans • The mapmaker has the camp plans.
• the crabs • • are • • in the lab • The crabs are in the lab.	• you • • said • • camp is a blast • You said camp is a blast.	• is that sap • • on the plant • Is that sap on the plant?
• the labs • • ran past • • the stamp plant • The labs ran past the stamp plant.	• Tam • • said • • to do your craft • Tam said to do your craft.	• Sam • • ran • • a fast lap • Sam ran a fast lap.

Exercise 6 · Masterpiece Sentences: Stage 1

▶ Use the diagrams in **Diagram It** (exercise 4) to write **Stage 1** base sentences. A base sentence is the same as a simple sentence.

1. _____

2. _____

3. _____

4. _____

5. _____

Exercise 1 · Name and Write

▸ Write the letters for the letter name your teacher says.

▸ Say the sound as you write the letter.

1. _____   3. _____   5. _____   7. _____   9. _____

2. _____   4. _____   6. _____   8. _____   10. _____

Exercise 2 · Sort It: Owner or Two or More

▶ Read each word.

1. crabs	**5.** ocean's	**9.** ants	**13.** bat's	**17.** tramp's
2. naps	**6.** oceans	**10.** Pat's	**14.** plans	**18.** rafts
3. river's	**7.** lamps	**11.** Stan's	**15.** clams	**19.** rat's
4. stamps	**8.** Fran's	**12.** cats	**16.** clam's	**20.** rats

▶ Copy the words in the correct column.

Owner	Two or More

Unit 2 · Lesson 7

Exercise 3 · Choose It and Use It

▸ Read the sentence with the blank and the bold word choices below it.

▸ Circle the word that correctly fits the blank.

▸ Write the word in the blank.

▸ Read the sentence again.

▸ Use that same word in a sentence of your own.

Note: Sentence answers will vary.

1. The raft is at _____ camp.

    Stan or Stan's

    _____

    _____

    _____

2. _____ map is at her camp by the ocean.

    Ann or Ann's

    _____

    _____

    _____

3. Fran has _____ of the ocean.

    map's or maps

    _____

    _____

    _____

(continued)

Exercise 3 (continued) · Choose It and Use It

4. _____ map of the ocean is damp.

   Sams or **Sam's**

   _____

   _____

   _____

5. The mapmaker's _____ sat on his maps.

   cats or **cat's**

   _____

   _____

   _____

Exercise 4 · Find It: Plural Nouns

▸ Look at **"A Map Is a Sandwich"** in the *Student Text,* pages 60–61.

▸ Find plural nouns.

▸ List them here.

_____

_____

_____

_____

_____

_____

Unit 2 · Lesson 7

Exercise 5 · Sentence Dictation

▶ Listen to each sentence.

▶ Repeat the sentence.

▶ Write it on the line.

▶ Circle the subject. Underline the predicate. Write "V" over the verb.

1. _____

2. _____

3. _____

4. _____

5. _____

▶ What do you notice about the predicate and the verb?

_____

_____

▶ Are these simple sentences?

_____

▶ How do you know?

_____

Exercise 6 · Sentence Morphs

▶ Practice scooping these phrases.

▶ Read as you would speak them.

• the plan • • is a trap • The plan is a trap.	• the scientist • • scans the plans • The scientist scans the plans.	• the labs • • ran past • • the stamp plant • The labs ran past the stamp plant.
• Sam • • ran • • a fast lap • Sam ran a fast lap.	• the mapmaker • • has the camp plans • The mapmaker has the camp plans.	• is that sap • • on the plant • Is that sap on the plant?
• the crabs • • are • • in the lab • The crabs are in the lab.	• Tam • • said • • to do your craft • Tam said to do your craft.	• you • • said • • camp is a blast • You said camp is a blast.

Exercise 1 · Sort It: Consonant Combinations

▸ Sort the words in the box by the beginning and ending consonant combinations.

clasp	ramp	clap	blast	cram
craft	clam	stamp	camp	past

▸ Write each word under the correct combination.

cl-	cr-	-mp	-st
_____	_____	_____	_____
_____	_____	_____	_____
_____	_____	_____	_____

Exercise 2 · Listening for Word Parts

▸ Listen to each word.

▸ Write the part your teacher repeats.

1. _____   3. _____   5. _____   7. _____   9. _____

2. _____   4. _____   6. _____   8. _____   10. _____

Exercise 3 · Introduction: Antonyms

▸ Write the antonym (opposite) for the word your teacher says.

1. _____   3. _____   5. _____

2. _____   4. _____

Exercise 4 · Diagram It: Subject/Predicate

▸ Add a predicate to the diagram to answer: What did it do?

▸ Write a sentence using the diagram.

1.   Who (or what) did it?   What did he do?

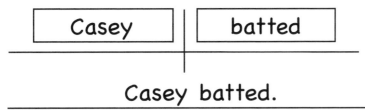

2.   Who (or what) did it?   What did she do?

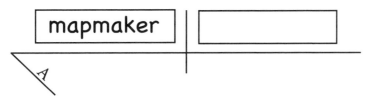

3.   Who (or what) did it?   What did it do?

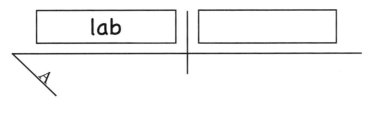

(continued)

Exercise 4 (continued) · Diagram It: Subject/Predicate

4.   Who (or what) did it?   What did they do?

| cast | | |

The

_____

5.   Who (or what) did it?   What did it do?

| plant | | |

The

_____

Exercise 5 · Instructional Text: "The Hardest Maps to Make"

▶ Listen as your teacher reads to you.

---

from "The Hardest Maps to Make"

Making maps is fun. We can see land. We can map it. We can map mountains. We can map plains. We can map valleys. But how about water? Can we map water—ponds, lakes, and rivers? Can we map oceans? Oceans are the hardest to map. They are deep. We can't see the bottom. It is dark. We can't take pictures. Fish can't talk to us. They can't share their travels.

▶ What short / *a* / words did you hear? Write them here.

_____

_____

Note: Use the *Student Text*, page 63, to answer the following questions.

1. What does **echo** mean?

_____

2. Why are echoes helpful to mapmakers?

_____

_____

Exercise 1 · Listening for Sounds in Words

▸ Put an X where you hear the sound.

1.

2.

3.

4.

5.

6.

7.

8.

9.

10.

Exercise 2 · Chain It

▸ Use your self-stick notes. Start with the word **flat**.

| f | l | a | t |

▸ Add or change the sound-spelling correspondence to make the next word your teacher says.

▸ Make a list of the words here:

_____

_____

_____

_____

_____

_____

_____

_____

_____

_____

Unit 2 · Lesson 9

Exercise 3 · Diagram It: Subject/Predicate

▶ Add a subject to the diagram to answer:

> Who (or what) did it?

▶ Write a sentence using the diagram.

1.

Who did it?	What did they do?
scientists	mapped

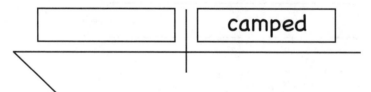

Scientists mapped.

2.

Who did it?	What did she do?
	planted

3.

Who (or what) did it?	What did he do?
	camped

(continued)

Exercise 3 (continued) · Diagram It: Subject/Predicate

4.   Who (or what) did it?   What did it do?

| | trapped |

5.   Who (or what) did it?   What did she do?

| | rafted |

Exercise 1 · Listening for Sounds in Words

▸ Write the letters for the sounds you hear in each word.

1. ⬜⬜⬜

2. ⬜⬜⬜

3. ⬜⬜⬜

4. ⬜⬜⬜

5. ⬜⬜⬜

6. ⬜⬜⬜⬜

7. ⬜⬜⬜⬜

8. ⬜⬜⬜⬜

9. ⬜⬜⬜⬜

10. ⬜⬜⬜⬜

Exercise 2 · Which Wall?

▶ Use the "**The Hardest Maps to Make**" **Blueprint for Writing** graphic organizers to find the right "wall" for the answer.

▶ Write the "wall" in the blank.

1. How did bats help mapmakers?

   Wall: _____

2. How do ocean maps help us?

   Wall: _____

3. How does sonar provide information?

   Wall: _____

4. What are the problems with sonar?

   Wall: _____

5. What do mapmakers want to know about the last frontier?

   Wall: _____

Unit 2 · Lesson 10

Exercise 3 · Using the Blueprint for Writing

▶ Use the **"The Hardest Maps to Make" Blueprint for Writing** graphic organizers to answer these questions.

1. How did bats help mapmakers?

_____

_____

2. How do ocean maps help us?

_____

_____

3. How does sonar provide information?

_____

_____

4. What are the problems with sonar?

_____

_____

5. What do mapmakers want to know about the last frontier?

_____

_____

Exercise 4 · Map It

▶ Use what you have learned about maps to make a map of your own.

▶ Include a base layer, detail, lines, color, and a map key.

Check off the activities you complete with each lesson. Evaluate your accomplishments at the end of each lesson. Pay attention to teacher evaluations and comments.

Unit Objectives	Lesson 1 (Date:_____)	Lesson 2 (Date:_____)
STEP 1 **Phonemic Awareness and Phonics** • Say the sounds for consonants **g**, **d**, and **v**. • Write letters for the sounds / g /, / d /, and / v /. • Say the short sound for the vowel **i**. • Write the letter for the short vowel sound / i /. • Identify syllables in spoken words.	❑ Move It and Mark It ❑ Phonemic Drills ❑ See and Say ❑ Exercise 1: Say and Write ❑ Exercise 2: Handwriting Practice	❑ Vowel Chart (T) ❑ Phonemic Drills ❑ See and Say ❑ Say and Write
STEP 2 **Word Recognition and Spelling** • Read and spell words with sound-spelling correspondences from this and previous units. • Build compound words. • Read and spell the **Essential Words**: *from, of, they, was, were, what*.	❑ Exercise 3: Spelling Pretest ❑ Build It, Bank It ❑ Memorize It	❑ Build It, Bank It ❑ Word Fluency 1 ❑ Memorize It ❑ Handwriting Practice
STEP 3 **Vocabulary and Morphology** • Define **Unit Vocabulary** words. • Identify and generate synonyms for **Unit Vocabulary**. • Use the word parts in compound words to determine meaning.	❑ Unit Vocabulary ❑ Multiple Meaning Map (T)	❑ Unit Vocabulary ❑ Exercise 1: Sort It
STEP 4 **Grammar and Usage** • Identify common and proper nouns. • Distinguish concrete and abstract nouns. • Identify the direct object in a sentence.	❑ Review: Multiple Functions of Words ❑ Exercise 4: Noun or Verb	❑ Introduction: Proper Nouns ❑ Find It (T)
STEP 5 **Listening and Reading** • Select the topic and details from informational text.	❑ Phrase Fluency 1 ❑ Exercise 5: Sentence Morphs	❑ Phrase Fluency 1 ❑ Exercise 2: Sentence Morphs ❑ Mini-Dialogs 1–4
STEP 6 **Speaking and Writing** • Generate sentences that present facts (statements). • Answer questions with **what**. • Record information on a graphic organizer.	❑ Masterpiece Sentences: Stage 1	❑ Masterpiece Sentences: Stage 1
Self-Evaluation (5 is the highest) 　**Effort** = I produced my best work. 　**Participation** = I was actively involved in tasks. 　**Independence** = I worked on my own.	**Effort:**　　1　2　3　4　5 **Participation:**　1　2　3　4　5 **Independence:**　1　2　3　4　5	**Effort:**　　1　2　3　4　5 **Participation:**　1　2　3　4　5 **Independence:**　1　2　3　4　5
Teacher Evaluation	**Effort:**　　1　2　3　4　5 **Participation:**　1　2　3　4　5 **Independence:**　1　2　3　4　5	**Effort:**　　1　2　3　4　5 **Participation:**　1　2　3　4　5 **Independence:**　1　2　3　4　5

(T) = Template

Lesson 3 (Date:_____)	**Lesson 4** (Date:_____)	**Lesson 5** (Date:_____)
❏ Consonant Chart (T) ❏ Phonemic Drills ❏ Exercise 1: Listening for Sounds in Words	❏ Review: Vowels and Consonants ❏ Phonemic Drills ❏ Exercise 1: Listening for Sounds in Words ❏ Letter-Sound Fluency	❏ Phonemic Drills ❏ Letter-Sound Fluency ❏ Exercise 1: Say and Write ❏ Content Mastery: Learning the Code
❏ Exercise 2: Listening for Word Parts ❏ Introduction: Words Ending in **v** ❏ Word Fluency 1 ❏ Exercise 3: Find It	❏ Chain It (T) ❏ Word Fluency 2 ❏ Type It ❏ Handwriting Practice	❏ Exercise 2: Sort It ❏ Content Mastery: Spelling Posttest 1
❏ Exercise 4: Word Networks: Antonyms	❏ Review: Singular Possessive Nouns and Plural Nouns ❏ Exercise 2: Find It ❏ Exercise 3: Sort It ❏ Exercise 4: Identify It	❏ Multiple Meaning Map (T)
❏ Exercise 5: Find It	❏ Exercise 5: Concrete and Abstract Nouns	❏ Review: Common, Proper, Concrete, and Abstract Nouns ❏ Exercise 3: Identify It: Nouns
❏ Mini-Dialogs 5–8 ❏ Exercise 6: Instructional Text: "Africa Digs"	❏ Instructional Text: "Africa Digs"	❏ Instructional Text: "Africa Digs"
❏ Exercise 7: Answer It ❏ Write Your Own Mini-Dialog (T)	❏ Exercise 6: Reading Response: "Africa Digs" ❏ Challenge Text: "The Big Dig"	❏ Reading Response: "Africa Digs" ❏ Challenge Text: "The Big Dig"
Effort: 1 2 3 4 5 **Participation:** 1 2 3 4 5 **Independence:** 1 2 3 4 5	**Effort:** 1 2 3 4 5 **Participation:** 1 2 3 4 5 **Independence:** 1 2 3 4 5	**Effort:** 1 2 3 4 5 **Participation:** 1 2 3 4 5 **Independence:** 1 2 3 4 5
Effort: 1 2 3 4 5 **Participation:** 1 2 3 4 5 **Independence:** 1 2 3 4 5	**Effort:** 1 2 3 4 5 **Participation:** 1 2 3 4 5 **Independence:** 1 2 3 4 5	**Effort:** 1 2 3 4 5 **Participation:** 1 2 3 4 5 **Independence:** 1 2 3 4 5

Lesson Checklist
Lessons 6–7

Check off the activities you complete with each lesson. Evaluate your accomplishments at the end of each lesson. Pay attention to teacher evaluations and comments.

Unit Objectives	Lesson 6 (Date:_____)	Lesson 7 (Date:_____)
STEP 1 — Phonemic Awareness and Phonics • Say the sounds for consonants <u>g</u>, <u>d</u>, and <u>v</u>. • Write letters for the sounds /g/, /d/, and /v/. • Say the short sound for the vowel <u>i</u>. • Write the letter for the short vowel sound /i/. • Identify syllables in spoken words.	❑ Review: Consonants and Vowels ❑ Review: Consonant Pairs ❑ Phonemic Drills ❑ Move It and Mark It ❑ See and Say ❑ Handwriting Practice	❑ Phonemic Drills ❑ See and Name ❑ Name and Write ❑ Listening for Sounds in Words ❑ Introduction: Syllables ❑ Syllable Awareness
STEP 2 — Word Recognition and Spelling • Read and spell words with sound-spelling correspondences from this and previous units. • Build compound words. • Read and spell the **Essential Words**: *from, of, they, was, were, what*.	❑ Exercise 1: Spelling Pretest ❑ Build It, Bank It ❑ Word Fluency 3	❑ Introduction: Compound Words ❑ Build It, Bank It
STEP 3 — Vocabulary and Morphology • Define **Unit Vocabulary** words. • Identify and generate synonyms for **Unit Vocabulary**. • Use the word parts in compound words to determine meaning.	❑ Review: Vocabulary ❑ Exercise 2: Classify It	❑ More About Compound Words ❑ Exercise 1: Find It ❑ Exercise 2: Choose It and Use It ❑ Exercise 3: Find It
STEP 4 — Grammar and Usage • Identify common and proper nouns. • Distinguish concrete and abstract nouns. • Identify the direct object in a sentence.	❑ Introduction: Direct Object ❑ Exercise 3: Code It ❑ Exercise 4: Diagram It	❑ Exercise 4: Sentence Dictation
STEP 5 — Listening and Reading • Select the topic and details from informational text.	❑ Phrase Fluency 2 ❑ Exercise 5: Sentence Morphs	❑ Phrase Fluency 2 ❑ Exercise 5: Sentence Morphs ❑ Mini-Dialogs 9–12
STEP 6 — Speaking and Writing • Generate sentences that present facts (statements). • Answer questions with **what**. • Record information on a graphic organizer.	❑ Exercise 6: Masterpiece Sentences: Stages 1 and 2	❑ Masterpiece Sentences: Stages 1 and 2 ❑ Write Your Own Mini-Dialog (T)
Self-Evaluation (5 is the highest) **Effort** = I produced my best work. **Participation** = I was actively involved in tasks. **Independence** = I worked on my own.	**Effort:** 1 2 3 4 5 **Participation:** 1 2 3 4 5 **Independence:** 1 2 3 4 5	**Effort:** 1 2 3 4 5 **Participation:** 1 2 3 4 5 **Independence:** 1 2 3 4 5
Teacher Evaluation	**Effort:** 1 2 3 4 5 **Participation:** 1 2 3 4 5 **Independence:** 1 2 3 4 5	**Effort:** 1 2 3 4 5 **Participation:** 1 2 3 4 5 **Independence:** 1 2 3 4 5

Lesson 8 (Date:_____)	**Lesson 9** (Date:_____)	**Lesson 10** (Date:_____)
❑ Phonemic Drills ❑ Letter-Name Fluency ❑ Exercise 1: Syllable Awareness	❑ Review: Vowel and Consonant Charts (T) ❑ Phonemic Drills ❑ Letter-Name Fluency ❑ Exercise 1: Syllable Awareness	❑ Exercise 1: Listening for Sounds in Words
❑ Review: Syllables ❑ Build It, Bank It ❑ Word Fluency 4	❑ Exercise 2: Listening for Word Parts ❑ Exercise 3: Build It	❑ Content Mastery: Spelling Posttest 2
❑ Exercise 2: Word Networks: Synonyms ❑ Content Mastery: Define It	❑ Multiple Meaning Map (T)	❑ Define It (T)
❑ Exercise 3: Diagram It	❑ Review: Nouns ❑ Exercise 4: Sentence Dictation	❑ Content Mastery: Subject or Direct Object
❑ Mini-Dialogs 13–16 ❑ Exercise 4: Instructional Text: "Africa Digs"	❑ Instructional Text: "Africa Digs" (T)	❑ Instructional Text: "Africa Digs" (T)
❑ Exercise 5: Answer It	❑ Blueprint for Writing (T) ❑ Challenge Text: "Dig This!"	❑ Exercise 2: Using the Blueprint for Writing ❑ Content Mastery: Reading Questions and Writing Answers ❑ Exercise 3: Challenge Text: "Dig This!"
Effort: 1 2 3 4 5 **Participation:** 1 2 3 4 5 **Independence:** 1 2 3 4 5	**Effort:** 1 2 3 4 5 **Participation:** 1 2 3 4 5 **Independence:** 1 2 3 4 5	**Effort:** 1 2 3 4 5 **Participation:** 1 2 3 4 5 **Independence:** 1 2 3 4 5
Effort: 1 2 3 4 5 **Participation:** 1 2 3 4 5 **Independence:** 1 2 3 4 5	**Effort:** 1 2 3 4 5 **Participation:** 1 2 3 4 5 **Independence:** 1 2 3 4 5	**Effort:** 1 2 3 4 5 **Participation:** 1 2 3 4 5 **Independence:** 1 2 3 4 5

Lesson 1

Exercise 1 · Say and Write

▸ Write the letter for each sound your teacher says.

▸ Say the sound as you write the letter.

1. _____   3. _____   5. _____   7. _____   9. _____

2. _____   4. _____   6. _____   8. _____   10. _____

Exercise 2 · Handwriting Practice

_____

_____

_____

_____

_____

_____

_____

_____

_____

Exercise 3 · Spelling Pretest

▶ Write the word your teacher repeats.

1. _____   6. _____

2. _____   7. _____

3. _____   8. _____

4. _____   9. _____

5. _____   10. _____

Exercise 4 · Noun or Verb

▶ Read the phrase.

▶ Decide if the word is a noun or verb.

▶ Circle your choice.

1. **dig** in your handbag	Noun	Verb
2. led a **dig**	Noun	Verb
3. a drill **bit**	Noun	Verb
4. **bit** the sandwich	Noun	Verb
5. **plant** the fig tree	Noun	Verb
6. a big **plant**	Noun	Verb
7. have a **fit**	Noun	Verb
8. **fit** it in the van	Noun	Verb
9. **flag** him in	Noun	Verb
10. hand the **flag**	Noun	Verb

Unit 3 · Lesson 1

Exercise 5 · Sentence Morphs

▸ Practice scooping these sentences.

▸ Read as you would speak them.

• I • • have a list • I have a list.	• They • • had the bone • • in the dig bag • They had the bone in the dig bag.	• That abstract print • • is a classic • That abstract print is a classic.
• The figs • • were big and fat • The figs were big and fat.	• I • • am at the Big Dig • I am at the Big Dig.	• They • • were at the dam • They were at the dam.
• Tim • • sat in the van • Tim sat in the van.	• Hans • • is from the Alps • Hans is from the Alps.	• Africa • • is a vast land • Africa is a vast land.

Exercise 1 · Sort It: People, Places, and Things

▸ Sort these words into categories.

I	rig	you	lip	lab	van
cab	they	flag	film	mitt	dad
pig	plant	camp	inn	hand	dam

▸ Write the words in the correct column.

▸ Some words are used more than once.

People	Places	Things

Exercise 2 · Sentence Morphs

▶ Practice scooping these sentences.

▶ Read as you would speak them.

• I • • have a list • I have a list.	• Africa • • is a vast land • Africa is a vast land.	• That abstract print • • is a classic • That abstract print is a classic.
• The figs • • were big and fat • The figs were big and fat.	• I • • am at the Big Dig • I am at the Big Dig.	• They • • had the bone • • in the dig bag • They had the bone in the dig bag.
• Tim • • sat in the van • Tim sat in the van.	• They • • were at the dam • They were at the dam.	• Hans • • is from the Alps • Hans is from the Alps.

Exercise 1 · Listening for Sounds in Words

▸ Put an X where you hear the short / *i* / sound.

1.

2.

3.

4.

5.

Exercise 2 · Listening for Word Parts

▸ Listen to each word.

▸ Write the part that your teacher repeats.

1. _____   6. _____

2. _____   7. _____

3. _____   8. _____

4. _____   9. _____

5. _____   10. _____

Exercise 3 · Find It: Essential Words

▸ Find the **Essential Words** for this unit in these sentences.

▸ Underline them.

▸ There may be more than one in a sentence.

▸ Circle the words that end with the / v / sound.

    1. They have six flags.

    2. What sad film did they give him?

    3. Bandits ran from the van.

    4. Traffic in Boston was bad.

    5. Granddad's bag of tidbits was in his hand.

    6. They were fit and trim.

    7. They live in Africa.

    8. The rabbit ran from the trap.

▸ Write the **Essential Words** in the spaces.

_____   _____   _____

_____   _____   _____

Exercise 4 · Word Networks: Antonyms

▸ Read the words in the box.

bad	dim
him	give
hit	live
in	grin
big	dad

▸ Select a word from the box that means the opposite (antonym) of each word your teacher says.

▸ Write the antonym on the line.

1. _____   6. _____

2. _____   7. _____

3. _____   8. _____

4. _____   9. _____

5. _____   10. _____

Unit 3 · Lesson 3

Exercise 5 · Find It: Subjects

▶ Listen and follow along as your teacher reads these sentences to you.

▶ Find the noun that is the subject—the word or words that answer:

> Who or what did it?

▶ Circle the noun that is the **subject.**

1. Dr. Paul Sereno led a dig.

2. 18 scientists went with him.

3. The Touareg have a legend.

4. The team takes the bones from the rock.

5. The bones are shipped.

6. The ship crosses the Atlantic Ocean.

7. The dinosaur's bones are cleaned.

8. *Jobaria* poses and looks real.

9. The dig's logbook sits on the table.

10. *Jobaria's* skeleton appears on the display.

▶ Sort the nouns.

Proper	Common	Possessive

Exercise 6 · Instructional Text: "Africa Digs"

▸ Listen as your teacher reads to you.

from "Africa Digs"

In 1997, Dr. Paul Sereno led a dig. He took 18 scientists with him. They went to Africa. They went to Niger. The Touareg tribe helped. The Touareg live in Niger. They know their land. They know it best. They made the dig possible.

Why did Dr. Sereno go to Niger? What did he hope to find? What was he digging for? Where did he dig? How long did he dig? What did he find? The Touareg have a legend. It tells of a giant animal. They call it *Jobar*.

The dig was a success. They had a fantastic find. They found a new species. It was a dinosaur. They called it *Jobaria* (giant). Come along. Let's watch their dig progress.

Step 1: We've Got One!

Touareg tribesmen lead. The team follows. They spot a special place. Bones stick out of desert rock. The Touareg tell a story. It is from their legend. These bones belong to the giant beast *Jobar*.

Step 2: Digging In

The dig begins. They use tools. They use hammers, chisels, and drills. They work for 10 weeks. A huge skeleton emerges. It is a dinosaur. How long has it been buried? 135 million years! 15 tons of rock cover it. The team takes the bones from the rock.

(continued)

Exercise 6 (continued) • Instructional Text: "Africa Digs"

1. What does the word **Touareg** mean? Underline context clues. Write a definition.

   _____

   _____

2. What short / *i* / words did you hear? Write them here.

   _____

   _____

Exercise 7 · Answer It

▸ Underline the person in your response for a "who" question.

▸ Underline the action or the name of a thing in your response for a "what" question.

1. Who led the dig in Niger, Africa?

_____

_____

2. Who lives in Niger?

_____

_____

3. Who helped Dr. Sereno with the dig?

_____

_____

4. What did the dig team find?

_____

_____

5. What is a legend?

_____

_____

Exercise 1 · Listening for Sounds in Words

▸ The letter **s** can represent two sounds: / s / and / z /.

> **Examples:**
>
> In **bats,** the **s** sounds like / s /.
>
> In **cabs,** the **s** sounds like / z /.

▸ Write the letters for the sounds in the words your teacher says.

▸ Circle the words in which the **s** sounds like / z /.

1.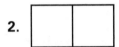

2. [ ][ ]

3. [ ][ ][ ]

4. [ ][ ][ ]

5. [ ][ ][ ]

6. [ ][ ][ ][ ]

7. [ ][ ][ ]

8. [ ][ ][ ][ ]

9. [ ][ ][ ]

10. [ ][ ][ ][ ]

Exercise 2 · Find It: Plural and Singular Possessive Nouns

▶ Listen to these sentences as your teacher reads.

▶ Underline the words that end with **-s** to mean more than one.

▶ Circle the words that end in **'s** to signal singular possession or ownership.

1. Dr. Sereno had plans for a dig in Africa.

2. Dr. Sereno's men had to sift sand for bones.

3. The men use tools to dig up dinosaur bones.

4. Some dinosaur bones stick out of rocks.

5. The dig's logbooks list the dinosaurs.

Unit 3 · Lesson 4

Exercise 3 · Sort It: Just One, The Owner, or Two or More

▸ Sort the nouns in the box into the correct columns below.

flag	dad's	films	digs	lamp's
snags	flag's	mints	gift	mitt
inn's	fig	lamps	hands	dam

▸ Match these terms with the columns. Write the correct term at the bottom of each column.

- Plural Nouns
- Possessive Singular Nouns
- Singular Nouns

Just One	The Owner	Two or More

Exercise 4 · Identify It: Singular, Singular Possessive, and Plural Nouns

▸ Read each sentence.

▸ Look at the underlined word.

▸ Identify if the underlined word is a **singular noun**, a **possessive singular noun**, or a **plural noun**.

▸ Mark your choice by putting an X in the correct box.

	Singular nouns		Plural nouns
Sentence	Singular Noun	Possessive Singular Noun	Plural Noun
1. The <u>rafts</u> land at Dan's camp.			
2. The lamp was in <u>Fran's</u> attic.			
3. The <u>crabs</u> dig in the sand.			
4. <u>Jim's</u> last trip to Africa was a blast.			
5. Brad had 10 <u>ribs</u> at the picnic.			
6. We dig for clams at <u>Sam's</u> picnic.			
7. Pam and Brad sift the damp <u>sand</u>.			
8. Brad gives <u>Dan's</u> rabbit to Hans.			
9. Stan's <u>cabin</u> is by the dam.			
10. Tim was a victim of <u>Pam's</u> bad plan.			

Unit 3 · Lesson 4

Exercise 5 · Concrete and Abstract Nouns

▸ Listen to the words your teacher says.

▸ Write **A** if the word is an abstract noun. Write **C** if the word is a concrete noun.

1. _____   6. _____

2. _____   7. _____

3. _____   8. _____

4. _____   9. _____

5. _____   10. _____

Exercise 6 · Reading Response: "Africa Digs"

▸ Start a logbook for **"Africa Digs."**

▸ Write one sentence for each step of the dig.

_____ **Logbook**

Step 1: _____

_____

Step 2: _____

_____

Step 3: _____

_____

Step 4: _____

_____

Step 5: _____

_____

Step 6: _____

_____

Lesson 5

Exercise 1 · Say and Write

▶ Write the letter for each sound your teacher says.

1. _____   3. _____   5. _____   7. _____   9. _____

2. _____   4. _____   6. _____   8. _____   10. _____

Exercise 2 · Sort It: Short Vowel Sounds

▶ Sort the words in the box by the short vowel sound you hear.

add	bit	pin	give	grand	jag
fib	band	flip	film	damp	grid
drab	print	valve	live	have	drag

▶ Write the word under the correct vowel sound.

short / *a* /	short / *i* /

Unit 3 · Lesson 5

Exercise 3 · Identify It: Nouns

▸ Listen to your teacher read this information to you.

---

from "Dig This!"

I was excited! I was going on a real <u>dig</u>! Would we find dinosaur <u>bones</u>?

1   2

I was a normal <u>10th grader</u>. For three <u>weeks</u> I got to be somebody special.

           3   4

I got to be a junior paleontologist. I got to hike in the <u>Rockies</u>. I got to visit

           5

the <u>Lewis and Clark Museum</u>. I got to make discoveries on <u>Egg Mountain</u>.

       6   7

I even got to do some <u>bird-watching</u>. Best of all, I made new <u>friends</u> and had

           8   9

lots of <u>fun</u>.

     10

▸ Put an X to show if the nouns are common or proper.

▸ Next put an X to show if the nouns are concrete or abstract.

	These nouns are		These nouns are	
	common	**proper**	**concrete**	**abstract**
1. dig				
2. bones				
3. 10th grader				
4. weeks				
5. Rockies				
6. Lewis and Clark Museum				
7. Egg Mountain				
8. bird-watching				
9. friends				
10. fun				

Exercise 1 · Spelling Pretest

▸ Write the word your teacher repeats.

1. _____   6. _____

2. _____   7. _____

3. _____   8. _____

4. _____   9. _____

5. _____   10. _____

Exercise 2 · Classify It

▸ Use **Unit Vocabulary** (page 77 in *Student Text*) and **Bank It** words.

▸ Find words that go together. Fill in the blanks.

1. _____ and _____ are both _____ .

2. _____ and _____ are both _____ .

3. _____ and _____ are both _____ .

4. _____ and _____ are both _____ .

5. _____ and _____ are both _____ .

Unit 3 · Lesson 6

Exercise 3 · Code It: Verbs and Direct Objects

▸ Listen to your teacher read each sentence.

▸ Write **V** over the verb in each sentence.

▸ Write **DO** over the direct object.

1. The team took the bones.

2. The team followed the Touareg tribe.

3. They spot a special place.

4. They use tools.

5. Dr. Sereno led the dig.

6. The jackets protect the fossils.

7. The scientists numbered the jackets.

8. Dr. Sereno kept the logbook.

9. The ship crosses the Atlantic.

10. The scientists build a dinosaur.

Exercise 4 · Diagram It: Subject/Predicate/Direct Object

▸ Fill in the diagrams with your teacher.

▸ Use sentence numbers 1, 4, 5, 6, and 7 from **Code It**.

1. Who did it?   What did it do?   What did it do it to?

    The / *the*

2. Who did it?   What did they do?   What did they do it to?

3. Who did it?   What did he do?   What did he do it to?

    the

4. What did it?   What did they do?   What did they do it to?

    The / *the*

5. Who did it?   What did they do?   What did they do it to?

    The / *the*

Unit 3 · Lesson 6

Exercise 5 · Sentence Morphs

▶ Practice scooping these phrases.

▶ Read as you would speak them.

I have a list. I have a list.	they were glad to have the facts They were glad to have the facts.	Lin and An were at a camp in Africa Lin and An were at a camp in Africa.
Hans was glad to have the grant Hans was glad to have the grant.	The Big Dig impacts traffic in Boston The Big Dig impacts traffic in Boston.	The limp flag flaps in the mist. The limp flag flaps in the mist.
do you have a stamp in your handbag Do you have a stamp in your handbag?	the traffic jam is in Boston The traffic jam is in Boston.	Jin and Alvis had to sprint to the bandstand Jin and Alvis had to sprint to the bandstand.

Exercise 6 · Masterpiece Sentences: Stages 1 and 2

▸ Use the information in this chart to write **Stage 2: Paint Your Predicate** sentences.

▸ Remember to use sentence signals—capital letters and periods.

Subject Who or what did it?	Predicate What did it or they do?	Direct Object What did they do it to?
Scientists	tagged	the bones
The dig team	cleaned	the fossils
Dr. Sereno	protected	each bone
The fabric strips	lifted	the skeleton

1. _____

2. _____

3. _____

4. _____

Exercise 1 · Find It: Singular Possessive and Plural Nouns

▸ Listen as the teacher reads the sentences.

▸ Circle the singular possessive nouns. Underline the plural nouns.

1. Brad's job in Boston made him glad.

2. But Boston's traffic jams were no picnic.

3. All the traffic gave him fits.

4. Big rigs sped past Brad's van.

5. He was timid on the ramps.

6. Traffic in the tunnels made him frantic.

7. He saw a lot of mishaps in the tunnels.

8. Brad's trips to his job were grim.

9. Brad had plans to slip out of Boston.

10. Bad mishaps on the tunnel's ramp made him miss the trip.

Exercise 2 · Choose It and Use It

▸ Read the sentence with the blank.

▸ Circle the word that correctly fits the blank.

▸ Write the word in the blank.

▸ Read the sentence again.

▸ Use that same word in a sentence of your own.

1. The _____ hid the tools in the victim's van.

       bandits or **bandit's**

_____

_____

_____

2. Brad and Dan grab the frantic _____ in the lab.

       rabbit's or **rabbits**

_____

_____

_____

3. They plan to use _____ script for the film.

       Al or **Al's**

_____

_____

_____

(continued)

Exercise 2 (continued) · Choose It and Use It

4. Dan has catnip _____ in the bag.

   plants or **plant's**

   _____

   _____

   _____

5. The cast has _____ script for this act.

   Jim's or **Jim**

   _____

   _____

   _____

Exercise 3 · Find It: Singular Possessive and Plural Nouns

▶ Review **"Africa Digs"** with your teacher.

▶ Identify the singular possessive nouns you find in Steps 5–9.

_____

_____

_____

▶ Identify the plural nouns you find in Steps 5–9.

_____

_____

_____

Unit 3 · Lesson 7

Exercise 4 · Sentence Dictation

▸ Listen to each sentence.

▸ Repeat the sentence.

▸ Write it on the line.

▸ Write **V** over the verb.

▸ Write **DO** over the direct object.

1. _____

2. _____

3. _____

4. _____

5. _____

Exercise 5 · Sentence Morphs

▸ Practice scooping these phrases.

▸ Read as you would speak them.

• I • • have a list • I have a list.	• they were glad • • to have • • the facts • They were glad to have the facts.	• do you • • have a stamp • • in your handbag • Do you have a stamp in your handbag?
• Hans • • was glad to have • • the land grant • Hans was glad to have the land grant.	• The Big Dig • • impacts traffic • • in Boston • The Big Dig impacts traffic in Boston.	• Lin and An • • were at a camp • • in Africa • Lin and An were at a camp in Africa.
• The limp flag • • flaps • • in the mist. • The limp flag flaps in the mist.	• the traffic jam • • is in Boston • The traffic jam is in Boston.	• Jin and Alvis • • had to sprint • • to the bandstand • Jin and Alvis had to sprint to the bandstand.

Exercise 1 · Syllable Awareness

▸ Listen to the word.

▸ Count the syllables.

▸ Write the letter for each vowel sound you hear.

	How many syllables do you hear?	1st Vowel Sound	2nd Vowel Sound	3rd Vowel Sound
1.				
2.				
3.				
4.				
5.				
6.				
7.				
8.				
9.				
10.				

Exercise 2 · Word Networks: Synonyms

▸ Write the synonym (same meaning) for the word your teacher says.

1. _____   3. _____   5. _____

2. _____   4. _____

Exercise 3 · Diagram It: Subject/Predicate/Direct Object

▶ Write a sentence using the diagram.

1.   Who did it?   What did she do?   What did she do it to?

The   the

_____

_____

2.   What did it?   What did it do?   What did it do it to?

The   the

_____

_____

3.   Who did it?   What did he do?   What did he do it to?

The   the

_____

_____

(continued)

Unit 3 · Lesson 8

4.   What did it?   What did it do?   What did it do it to?

        The   *the*

5.   What did it?   What did it do?   What did it do it to?

        The   *the*

Exercise 4 · Instructional Text: "Africa Digs"

What Do I Know So Far?

▸ Listen as your teacher reads these questions to you.

1. Where does the dig begin?

_____

2. What do I know about the region?

_____

3. Write one word that you think of for these vocabulary words:

Niger: _____

desert: _____

fossil: _____

dinosaur: _____

Unit 3 · Lesson 8

Exercise 5 · Answer It

▸ Underline the person in your response for a "who" question.

▸ Underline the action or the name of a thing in your response for a "what" question.

1. What did the dig team make to protect the fossils?

   _____

   _____

2. What did they use to move the tons of bones?

   _____

   _____

3. What did they use to clean the bones?

   _____

   _____

Lesson 9

Exercise 1 · Syllable Awareness

▶ Listen to the word.

▶ Count the syllables.

▶ Write the letter for each vowel sound you hear.

	How many syllables do you hear?	1st Vowel Sound	2nd Vowel Sound	3rd Vowel Sound
1.				
2.				
3.				
4.				
5.				
6.				
7.				
8.				
9.				
10.				

Unit 3 · Lesson 9

Exercise 2 · Listening for Word Parts

▸ Listen to each word.

▸ Write the word part your teacher repeats.

1. _____   3. _____   5. _____   7. _____   9. _____

2. _____   4. _____   6. _____   8. _____   10. _____

Exercise 3 · Build It

▸ Use the syllables above to build two-syllable words. Write them on the lines.

_____

_____

_____

_____

_____

Exercise 4 · Sentence Dictation

▸ Listen to each sentence.

▸ Repeat the sentence.

▸ Write it on the line.

▸ Add a direct object to the sentence.

1. _____

2. _____

3. _____

4. _____

5. _____

Lesson 10

Exercise 1 · Listening for Sounds in Words

▸ Write the letters for the sounds you hear in each word.

1.

2.

3.

4.

5.

6.

7.

8.

9.

10.

Unit 3 · Lesson 10

Exercise 2 · Using the Blueprint for Writing

▸ Use the graphic organizer for **"Africa Digs"** to identify which wall would be helpful to answer these questions. Write the name of the wall on the line.

1. What did they find on the dig?

   _____

   _____

2. How did the scientists transport the bones?

   _____

   _____

3. What did the scientists do to protect the fossils?

   _____

   _____

4. How do scientists discover missing bones?

   _____

   _____

5. How do scientists reconstruct the dinosaur?

   _____

   _____

Exercise 3 · Challenge Text: "Dig This!"

▸ Compare **"Africa Digs"** and **"Dig This!"** and fill in the chart.

Connect Text		
Africa Digs	**Both**	**Dig This!**

Check off the activities you complete with each lesson. Evaluate your accomplishments at the end of each lesson. Pay attention to teacher evaluations and comments.

Unit Objectives	Lesson 1 (Date:_____)	Lesson 2 (Date:_____)
STEP 1 **Phonemic Awareness and Phonics** • Say the sounds for consonants <u>w</u>, <u>y</u>, <u>z</u>, and <u>k</u>. • Write letters for sounds / w /, / y /, / z /, and / k /. • Say the short sound for the vowel <u>i</u>. • Write the letter for the short vowel sound / i /. • Identify syllables in spoken words.	❑ Move It and Mark It ❑ Phonemic Drills ❑ See and Say ❑ Exercise 1: Say and Write ❑ Exercise 2: Handwriting Practice	❑ Consonant Chart (T) ❑ Phonemic Drills ❑ See and Say
STEP 2 **Word Recognition and Spelling** • Read and spell words with sound-spelling correspondences from this and previous units. • Read and spell the **Essential Words:** *be, does, he, she, we, when*.	❑ Exercise 3: Spelling Pretest ❑ Build It, Bank It ❑ Memorize It	❑ Exercise 1: Sort It ❑ Word Fluency 1 ❑ Memorize It ❑ Handwriting Practice
STEP 3 **Vocabulary and Morphology** • Define **Unit Vocabulary** words. • Identify and generate synonyms and antonyms for **Unit Vocabulary** words. • Define and use idioms. • Add **-s** to verbs to signal third person singular present tense.	❑ Unit Vocabulary ❑ Multiple Meaning Map (T)	❑ Introduction: Third Person Singular Present Tense Verb Ending ❑ Exercise 2: Find It ❑ Exercise 3: Rewrite It ❑ Exercise 4: Identify It
STEP 4 **Grammar and Usage** • Identify nominative (subject) pronouns. • Identify prepositions and prepositional phrases. • Identify present tense verbs. • Identify adverbs as part of the predicate.	❑ Introduction: Pronouns ❑ Exercise 4: Rewrite It: Pronouns	❑ More About Pronouns ❑ Exercise 5: Rewrite It: Pronouns
STEP 5 **Listening and Reading** • Select the topic and details from informational text.	❑ Phrase Fluency 1 ❑ Exercise 5: Sentence Morphs	❑ Decodable Text: "Facts About Twins" Mega-Dialog ❑ Sentence Fluency 1
STEP 6 **Speaking and Writing** • Generate sentences that present facts (statements). • Answer questions with **when**. • Record information on a graphic organizer.	❑ Masterpiece Sentences: Stages 1 and 2	❑ Masterpiece Sentences: Stages 1 and 2
Self-Evaluation (5 is the highest) **Effort** = I produced my best work. **Participation** = I was actively involved in tasks. **Independence** = I worked on my own.	**Effort:** 1 2 3 4 5 **Participation:** 1 2 3 4 5 **Independence:** 1 2 3 4 5	**Effort:** 1 2 3 4 5 **Participation:** 1 2 3 4 5 **Independence:** 1 2 3 4 5
Teacher Evaluation	**Effort:** 1 2 3 4 5 **Participation:** 1 2 3 4 5 **Independence:** 1 2 3 4 5	**Effort:** 1 2 3 4 5 **Participation:** 1 2 3 4 5 **Independence:** 1 2 3 4 5

Lesson 3 (Date:_____)	Lesson 4 (Date:_____)	Lesson 5 (Date:_____)
❑ Review: Consonants and Vowels ❑ Phonemic Drills ❑ Exercise 1: Listening for Sounds in Words	❑ Review: Consonant Sounds ❑ Phonemic Drills ❑ Exercise 1: Listening for Sounds in Words ❑ Letter-Sound Fluency	❑ Phonemic Drills ❑ Letter-Sound Fluency ❑ Exercise 1: Say and Write ❑ Content Mastery: Learning the Code
❑ Exercise 2: Listening for Word Parts ❑ Word Fluency 1 ❑ Exercise 3: Find It	❑ Chain It ❑ Word Fluency 2 ❑ Type It ❑ Handwriting Practice	❑ Content Mastery: Spelling Posttest 1 ❑ Exercise 2: Sort It
❑ Exercise 4: Word Networks: Antonyms ❑ Introduction: Idioms ❑ Draw It	❑ More About Third Person Singular Present Tense Endings ❑ Exercise 2: Identify It ❑ Exercise 3: Rewrite It	❑ Multiple Meaning Map (T)
❑ Introduction: Prepositions ❑ Exercise 5: Find It	❑ Introduction: Adverbs ❑ Exercise 4: Sort It	❑ More About Adverbs ❑ Masterpiece Sentences: Stage 2
❑ Decodable Text: "Facts About Twins" ❑ Mega-Dialog ❑ Exercise 6: Instructional Text: "Remarkable Twins"	❑ Instructional Text: "Remarkable Twins"	❑ Instructional Text: "Remarkable Twins"
❑ Exercise 7: Answer It	❑ Exercise 5: Reading Response: "Remarkable Twins" ❑ Challenge Text: "Conjoined Twins"	❑ Exercise 3: Reading Response: "Remarkable Twins" ❑ Challenge Text: "Conjoined Twins"
Effort: 1 2 3 4 5 **Participation:** 1 2 3 4 5 **Independence:** 1 2 3 4 5	**Effort:** 1 2 3 4 5 **Participation:** 1 2 3 4 5 **Independence:** 1 2 3 4 5	**Effort:** 1 2 3 4 5 **Participation:** 1 2 3 4 5 **Independence:** 1 2 3 4 5
Effort: 1 2 3 4 5 **Participation:** 1 2 3 4 5 **Independence:** 1 2 3 4 5	**Effort:** 1 2 3 4 5 **Participation:** 1 2 3 4 5 **Independence:** 1 2 3 4 5	**Effort:** 1 2 3 4 5 **Participation:** 1 2 3 4 5 **Independence:** 1 2 3 4 5

Check off the activities you complete with each lesson. Evaluate your accomplishments at the end of each lesson. Pay attention to teacher evaluations and comments.

	Unit Objectives	Lesson 6 (Date:_____)	Lesson 7 (Date:_____)
STEP 1	**Phonemic Awareness and Phonics** • Say the sounds for consonants <u>w</u>, <u>y</u>, <u>z</u>, and <u>k</u>. • Write letters for sounds / w /, / y /, / z /, and / k /. • Say the short sound for the vowel <u>i</u>. • Write the letter for the short vowel sound / i /.	❑ Review: Consonants and Vowels ❑ Review: Voiceless and Voiced Consonant Pairs ❑ Phonemic Drills ❑ Move It and Mark It ❑ See and Say ❑ Handwriting Practice	❑ Phonemic Drills ❑ See and Name ❑ Name and Write ❑ Listening for Sounds in Words ❑ Review: Syllables ❑ Syllable Awareness
STEP 2	**Word Recognition and Spelling** • Read and spell words with sound-spelling correspondences from this and previous units. • Read and spell the **Essential Words:** *be, does, he, she, we, when.*	❑ Exercise 1: Spelling Pretest ❑ Build It, Bank It ❑ Word Fluency 3	❑ Review: Compound Words ❑ Build It, Bank It
STEP 3	**Vocabulary and Morphology** • Define **Unit Vocabulary** words. • Identify and generate synonyms and antonyms for **Unit Vocabulary** words. • Define and use idioms. • Add **-s** to verbs to signal third person singular present tense.	❑ Review: Vocabulary ❑ Exercise 2: Classify It	❑ More About Compound Words ❑ Exercise 1: Identify It ❑ Exercise 2: Verb or Noun
STEP 4	**Grammar and Usage** • Identify nominative (subject) pronouns. • Identify prepositions and prepositional phrases. • Identify present tense verbs. • Identify adverbs as part of the predicate.	❑ Introduction: Predicate Expansion With Adverbs ❑ Exercise 3: Code It ❑ Exercise 4: Diagram It	❑ Exercise 3: Sentence Dictation
STEP 5	**Listening and Reading** • Select the topic and details from informational text.	❑ Phrase Fluency 2 ❑ Exercise 5: Sentence Morphs	❑ Decodable Text: "The Vast Sky" Mega-Dialog ❑ Sentence Fluency 2
STEP 6	**Speaking and Writing** • Generate sentences that present facts (statements). • Answer questions with **when**. • Record information on a graphic organizer.	❑ Masterpiece Sentences: Stages 1 and 2	❑ Exercise 4: Masterpiece Sentences: Stages 1 and 2
	Self-Evaluation (5 is the highest) **Effort** = I produced my best work. **Participation** = I was actively involved in tasks. **Independence** = I worked on my own.	**Effort:** 1 2 3 4 5 **Participation:** 1 2 3 4 5 **Independence:** 1 2 3 4 5	**Effort:** 1 2 3 4 5 **Participation:** 1 2 3 4 5 **Independence:** 1 2 3 4 5
	Teacher Evaluation	**Effort:** 1 2 3 4 5 **Participation:** 1 2 3 4 5 **Independence:** 1 2 3 4 5	**Effort:** 1 2 3 4 5 **Participation:** 1 2 3 4 5 **Independence:** 1 2 3 4 5

Lesson Checklist
Lessons 8–10

Lesson 8 (Date:_____)	**Lesson 9** (Date:_____)	**Lesson 10** (Date:_____)
❑ Phonemic Drills ❑ Letter-Name Fluency ❑ Exercise 1: Syllable Awareness	❑ Review: Vowel and Consonant Charts (T) ❑ Phonemic Drills ❑ Letter-Name Fluency ❑ Exercise 1: Syllable Awareness	❑ Exercise 1: Listening for Sounds in Words
❑ Review: Syllables ❑ Exercise 2: Sort It ❑ Word Fluency 4	❑ Exercise 2: Listening for Word Parts ❑ Exercise 3: Build It, Bank It	❑ Content Mastery: Spelling Posttest 2
❑ Exercise 3: Word Networks: Synonyms ❑ Content Mastery: Define It	❑ Multiple Meaning Map (T)	❑ Draw It ❑ Define It (T)
❑ Exercise 4: Diagram It ❑ Exercise 5: Tense Timeline	❑ Review: Predicate Expansion ❑ Exercise 4: Sentence Dictation	❑ Content Mastery: Pronouns, Prepositions, and Adverbs
❑ Decodable Text: "The Vast Sky" Mega-Dialog ❑ Instructional Text: "Gemini: The Twins"	❑ Instructional Text: "Gemini: The Twins" (T)	❑ Instructional Text: "Gemini: The Twins" (T)
❑ Answer It ❑ Exercise 6: Reading Response: "Gemini: The Twins"	❑ Blueprint for Writing (T) ❑ Challenge Text: "Twin Towers: Two Perspectives"	❑ Blueprint for Writing (T) ❑ Challenge Text: "Twin Towers: Two Perspectives"
Effort: 1 2 3 4 5 **Participation:** 1 2 3 4 5 **Independence:** 1 2 3 4 5	**Effort:** 1 2 3 4 5 **Participation:** 1 2 3 4 5 **Independence:** 1 2 3 4 5	**Effort:** 1 2 3 4 5 **Participation:** 1 2 3 4 5 **Independence:** 1 2 3 4 5
Effort: 1 2 3 4 5 **Participation:** 1 2 3 4 5 **Independence:** 1 2 3 4 5	**Effort:** 1 2 3 4 5 **Participation:** 1 2 3 4 5 **Independence:** 1 2 3 4 5	**Effort:** 1 2 3 4 5 **Participation:** 1 2 3 4 5 **Independence:** 1 2 3 4 5

Exercise 1 · Say and Write

▸ Write the letter or letters for each sound your teacher says.

▸ Say the sound as you write the letter.

1. _____   3. _____   5. _____   7. _____   9. _____

2. _____   4. _____   6. _____   8. _____   10. _____

Exercise 2 · Handwriting Practice

_____

_____

_____

_____

_____

_____

Exercise 3 · Spelling Pretest

1. _____   6. _____

2. _____   7. _____

3. _____   8. _____

4. _____   9. _____

5. _____   10. _____

Exercise 4 · Rewrite It: Pronouns

▸ Read the pronouns in the box.

I	he	it	you
you	she	we	they

▸ Read the sentence and underline the subject.

▸ Replace the subject with a pronoun.

▸ Rewrite the sentence using the pronoun.

▸ Circle the pronoun in your sentence.

1. Jack gives the can a swift kick.

_____

2. Kim and Kari live on a ranch.

_____

3. Kim gave her twin a pat on the back.

_____

4. Granddad and I packed for a picnic.

_____

5. The yak had a pack on its back.

_____

Exercise 5 · Sentence Morphs

▸ Practice scooping these sentences.

▸ Read as you would speak them.

His pad was Graceland **His pad was Graceland.**	Ask a fan if he lives **Ask a fan if he lives!**	Elvis and his twin were born in 1935 **Elvis and his twin were born in 1935.**
Fans "flip their lids" for him **Fans "flip their lids" for him.**	Elvis was in hit films **Elvis was in hit films.**	The twins admit they are pals **The twins admit they are pals.**
The twins have a pack of pets **The twins have a pack of pets.**	The twins have cats and a pig **The twins have cats and a pig.**	Kim is a big fan of her twin **Kim is a big fan of her twin.**

Exercise 1 · Sort It: Spelling / k /

▸ Sort the words in the box by the position of the / k / sound and how the sound is spelled.

cat	ask	kit	pick	snack
kid	cab	brick	cast	brisk
pack	disk	task	kin	mask

▸ Write the words in the correct column.

c-	k-	-ck	-k

Unit 4 · Lesson 2

Exercise 2 · Find It: Third Person Singular Verb Ending

▶ Listen as your teacher reads the sentences out loud.

▶ Underline the verbs that end with <u>s</u>. The -**s** on the verb signals present tense.

1. Elvis twists like a cat in a can of catnip.

2. Elvis snacks on a stack of flapjacks.

3. The famous man sips a big glass of milk.

4. That twin sprints as fast as the wind.

5. He runs as fast as a rabbit.

6. She sprints at the track.

7. He wins the big event.

8. Kim lives with her twin sister, Kari.

9. Kim gabs with her twin, Kari.

10. Kari trims the horse's mane.

Exercise 3 · Rewrite It: Third Person Singular Verb Ending

▸ Read each sentence out loud.

▸ Change the underlined verb by adding **-s** to signal third person singular present tense.

▸ Restate the sentence.

▸ Rewrite the sentence with the changed verb.

Add -s	Copy the sentence
Example: Elvis <u>kick**S**</u>.	**Example:** Elvis kicks.
1. Jack <u>snack</u>.	**1.** _____
2. Alvin <u>win</u>.	**2.** _____
3. Casey <u>swim</u>.	**3.** _____
4. Tam <u>skim</u>.	**4.** _____
5. Kim <u>crack</u> up.	**5.** _____
6. Kari <u>skip</u> in.	**6.** _____
7. Kari <u>win</u> the pig.	**7.** _____
8. Kim's pig <u>swim</u> fast.	**8.** _____
9. Elvis <u>give</u> Kim a hand.	**9.** _____
10. Tim <u>stack</u> the twigs out back.	**10.** _____

Unit 4 · Lesson 2

Exercise 4 · Identify It: Singular, Possessive, or Present Tense

▶ Read each sentence.

▶ Look at the underlined word.

▶ Decide if the underlined word is a:

- Singular noun (**pig**, **cab**, **Kim**).

- Possessive singular noun (**pig**'s back, **cab**'s mat, **Kim**'s mask).

- Present tense verb (Kim **lifts**, she **packs**).

▶ Write an X to mark your choice.

Sentence	Noun		Verb
	Singular Noun	Possessive Singular Noun (The Owner)	Present Tense
Example: Kim <u>asks</u> the twins for skim milk.			X
1. Jack's van <u>skids</u> on the ramp.			
2. Fran gives <u>milk</u> to his black cats.			
3. Kim <u>swims</u> fast.			
4. Nick twists <u>Kim's</u> napkin.			
5. A black tick bit <u>Brad's</u> twin.			
6. Liz <u>yaks</u> about her win.			
7. We lift the pack onto the <u>yak's</u> back.			
8. <u>Tim's</u> back cracks when he puts packs on his yaks.			
9. Brad <u>packs</u> his swim bag with snacks.			
10. Elvis camps on his <u>land</u>.			

Exercise 5 · Rewrite It: Pronouns

▶ Read the sentence and underline the subject.

▶ Replace the subject with a pronoun.

▶ Rewrite the sentence using the pronoun.

▶ Circle the pronoun in your sentences.

▶ Fill in the chart with the circled pronouns.

1. The twins were at the track.

_____

2. Elvis was in hit films.

_____

3. Kim is a big fan of her twin.

_____

4. The twins and I ran fast at the track.

_____

5. The black asp slid on the twig.

_____

Person	Number	
	Singular	**Plural**
First Person	I	
Second Person	you	you
Third Person		

Exercise 1 · Listening for Sounds in Words

▸ Put an X where you hear the / k / sound.

▸ If you do not hear / k /, write the letters for the sounds in the boxes.

1.
2.
3.
4.
5.
6.
7.
8.
9.
10.

Exercise 2 · Listening for Word Parts

▶ Listen to each word.

▶ Write the part that your teacher repeats.

1. _____   6. _____

2. _____   7. _____

3. _____   8. _____

4. _____   9. _____

5. _____   10. _____

Exercise 3 · Find It: Essential Words

▶ Find the Unit 4 **Essential Words** in these sentences.

▶ Underline them. (There may be more than one in a sentence.)

1. He is a remarkable twin.

2. When did the twins win?

3. We are Elvis fans.

4. Does she have a twin?

5. It is remarkable to be a twin!

▶ Write the **Essential Words** in the spaces.

_____   _____

_____   _____

_____   _____

▶ Circle the four **Essential Words** that rhyme.

Unit 4 · Lesson 3

Exercise 4 · Word Networks: Antonyms

▶ Read the words in the box.

he	abstract	black	back	ask
zigzag	swim	sick	win	kid

▶ Select the antonym, or opposite, for the word your teacher says.

1. _____   6. _____

2. _____   7. _____

3. _____   8. _____

4. _____   9. _____

5. _____   10. _____

Exercise 5 · Find It: Prepositions

▸ Listen and follow along as your teacher reads these sentences to you.

▸ Underline the preposition.

▸ Circle the object of the preposition (noun).

▸ Read the prepositional phrase.

▸ List the prepositions on the line below the sentences.

1. Elvis Presley was born in 1935.

2. Elvis was born in Mississippi.

3. Jesse died at birth.

4. Elvis spoke of his twin.

5. Elvis died at Graceland.

6. Can you tell Kari from Kim?

7. The twins lived on a ranch.

8. Kari and Kim moved to Florida.

9. Mark and Scott Kelly grew up in New Jersey.

10. The Kellys were the first twins to fly into space.

Prepositions: _____

Unit 4 · Lesson 3

Exercise 6 · Instructional Text: "Remarkable Twins"

▸ Listen to these sentences. Think about the meaning of **record** in each one. Discuss with the class.

1. Elvis sold more **records** than anyone.

2. A **record** is a round disk that plays music on a record player.

3. Twins set **records** for doing remarkable things.

4. A **record** is a written account of the highest achievement in a competition.

Exercise 7 · Answer It

▸ Write the answer to each question.

▸ Underline the time information in your response for the "when" question.

1. When was Elvis born? When did Jesse die?

   _____

2. When did Elvis get a guitar?

   _____

▸ Write two "when" questions in the blanks below.

   _____

   _____

Exercise 1 · Listening for Sounds in Words

▸ The letter **s** can represent two sounds: / s / and / z /.

> **Examples:**
>
> In **bats**, the **s** sounds like / s /.
>
> In **bags**, the **s** sounds like / z /.

▸ Write the letters for the sounds in the words your teacher says.

▸ Circle the words in which the **s** sounds like / z /.

1. ☐☐☐☐

2. ☐☐☐☐

3. ☐☐☐☐

4. ☐☐☐☐

5. ☐☐☐

6. ☐☐☐

7. ☐☐☐☐

8. ☐☐☐☐

9. ☐☐☐☐

10. ☐☐☐☐

Unit 4 · Lesson 4

Exercise 2 · Identify It: Pronouncing -s

▸ Add the third person present tense singular ending to the verbs. (She zip**s**.)

▸ Copy the third person present tense singular form of the verb. Say the sound of each letter as you write it.

▸ Read the third person present tense singular verb out loud.

▸ Identify if the **s** sounds like / s / or / z /.

Add the suffix -s	Copy the word with the ending	Does **s** sound like . . .	
		/ s /	/ z /
Example 1: stack **S**	stacks	X	
Example 2: dig **S**	digs		X
1. ask_____			
2. snag_____			
3. crack_____			
4. flick_____			
5. lick_____			
6. skid_____			
7. pack_____			
8. mask_____			
9. skim_____			
10. stand_____			

Exercise 3 · Rewrite It: Match Nouns and Verbs

▶ Read the sentence in the first column. The underlined word is the subject. It is a plural (two or more) noun or pronoun.

▶ Circle the verb in each sentence.

▶ Read the sentence in the second column. The plural subject has been changed to a singular (just one) subject.

▶ Change the form of the verb into the third person singular present tense. Write the verb in the blank.

▶ Read the sentence to check your answer.

Third person plural subjects, present tense verbs.	Third person singular subjects, present tense verbs.
Examples: The kids (lick) the stamps. They (snack) on the dock.	**Examples:** She ____licks____ the stamps. He ____snacks____ on the dock.
1. The cats lick the milk.	1. The cat _____ the milk.
2. They stack bricks on the dock.	2. She _____ bricks on the dock.
3. The vans skid into the twin's cabin.	3. The van _____ into the twin's cabin.
4. The twins snack on crabs and clams.	4. He _____ on crabs and clams.
5. The black yaks swim in a zigzag.	5. The black yak _____ in a zigzag.
6. They admit the victim into the clinic.	6. He _____ the victim into the clinic.
7. Hanif's clocks tick in the cabin.	7. Hanif's clock _____ in the cabin.
8. The bandits jack up the van.	8. He _____ up the van.
9. The twins pick up the napkins for the picnic.	9. A twin _____ up the napkins for the picnic.
10. The crash victims panic.	10. The crash victim _____ .

Exercise 4 · Sort It: When, Where, or How

▸ Listen to the selection.

▸ Decide if the underlined words and phrases tell **when, where,** or **how.**

▸ Write the words or phrases in the correct template column on the following page.

Elvis and Jesse Presley
Kim and Kari Baker
based on "Remarkable Twins"

Elvis Presley was born a twin in 1935 <u>in Mississippi</u>. <u>Unfortunately,</u> his twin Jesse died <u>at birth</u>. Elvis became famous. He went on to make music history. He got his start in music, when he got a guitar <u>for Christmas in 1946</u>. <u>From that beginning,</u> Elvis went on to sell more records than anyone.

Kim and Kari Baker are also twins. They were born <u>in Montana</u>. These twins are ranchers and photographers. Born in Montana, they lived there <u>until their teens</u>, when they moved <u>to Florida</u>. There they developed a love for horses. <u>In 1988</u>, they returned to Montana and became ranchers. Their love of horses continues. <u>Remarkably,</u> horses can tell them apart, but people often can't!

(continued)

Exercise 4 (continued) · Sort It: When, Where, or How

When	Where	How

Unit 4 · Lesson 4

Exercise 5 · Reading Response: "Remarkable Twins"

▸ Write the answers to these questions.

▸ Use information from the **"Kim and Kari Baker"** section of **"Remarkable Twins."**

▸ Write a phrase or sentence to answer each question.

1. Who did it?

_____

2. What did they do?

_____

3. How did they make history?

_____

_____

4. Why are they remarkable?

_____

_____

▸ Combine these answers to write a paragraph.

_____

_____

_____

_____

_____

_____

Exercise 1 · Say and Write

▸ Repeat each sound your teacher says.

▸ Write the letter or letters that represent the sound.

1. _____ 3. _____ 5. _____ 7. _____ 9. _____

2. _____ 4. _____ 6. _____ 8. _____ 10. _____

Unit 4 · Lesson 5

Exercise 2 · Sort It: Spellings for / k /

▶ Sort the words in the box according to the spelling for / k /.

cat	kick	milk	wick	cast	kin
silk	Jack	cab	clip	clack	risk
click		kit		kid	

▶ Write each word under the correct spelling for / k /. (Some words can be in more than one cell.)

c-	k-	cl-

~ck	-lk	-sk

Exercise 3 · Reading Response: "Remarkable Twins"

▶ Work with a partner and write the answers to these questions.

▶ Use information from your choice of **"Remarkable Twins"** on pages 134–137 in the *Student Text*.

1. Who did it? _____

2. What did they do? _____

3. Where? _____

4. When? _____

▶ Combine answers 1–4 to write a **Masterpiece Sentence** about the twins.

_____

_____

▶ Now, answer these questions.

5. How did they make history?

_____

6. Why are they remarkable?

_____

▶ Combine answers 5 and 6 with the **Masterpiece Sentence** to write a paragraph.

_____

_____

_____

_____

_____

Exercise 1 · Spelling Pretest

▶ Write the words your teacher says.

1. _____   6. _____

2. _____   7. _____

3. _____   8. _____

4. _____   9. _____

5. _____   10. _____

Exercise 2 · Classify It

▶ Use **Unit Vocabulary** (page 115 in *Student Text*) and **Bank It** words.

▶ Find words that go together. Fill in the blanks.

1. _____ and _____ are both _____ .

2. _____ and _____ are both _____ .

3. _____ and _____ are both _____ .

4. _____ and _____ are both _____ .

5. _____ and _____ are both _____ .

Exercise 3 · Code It: Verbs and Adverbs

▸ Listen to your teacher read each sentence.

Part A: Write **V** over the verb in each sentence.

1. The twins ran at the track.

2. The twig snaps in the wind.

3. The stars sparkle at night.

4. The constellations shine brightly.

5. The damp wind blew during the storm.

Part B: Underline adverbs or prepositional phrases that act as adverbs. Write **ADV** over the word or words you underline.

6. The tracks led to the attic.

7. That yak has ticks on its back.

8. The cast performed Saturday night.

9. Casey hit last.

10. The towers fell in September.

Unit 4 · Lesson 6

Exercise 4 · Diagram It: Subject / Predicate

▸ Fill in the first sentence diagram with your teacher.

▸ Diagram sentence numbers 2, 3, 9, and 10 from **Code It** (exercise 3).

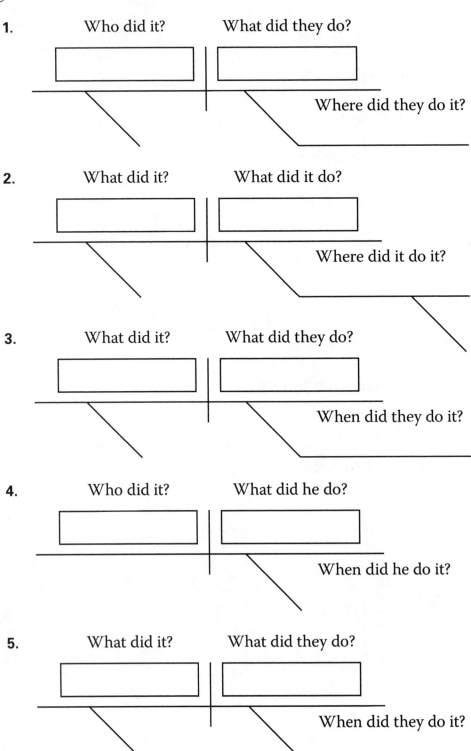

Exercise 5 · Sentence Morphs

▸ Practice scooping these sentences.

▸ Read as you would speak them.

They map the stars They map the stars.	Its name was the twin plants Its name was the twin plants.	The twin is in the vast sky The twin is in the vast sky.
They used them to plan trips They used them to plan trips.	They map the stars They map the stars.	A man can plant sprigs A man can plant sprigs.
His task is to scan the sky His task is to scan the sky.	His task is to name the stars His task is to name the stars.	It is used to transmit facts It is used to transmit facts.

Exercise 1 · Identify It: Word Forms With -s

▶ Identify the underlined *nouns*:

1. *Singular*
2. *Plural*
3. *Singular Possessive*

▶ Identify the underlined *present tense verbs*:

1. *Third person singular form*
2. *Other person and plural form*

Sentences	Nouns			Present Tense Verbs	
	Singular	Plural	Singular Possessive	Third Person Singular Form	Other Person and Plural Form
Example: <u>Kim's</u> twin is also a star.			X		
Example: He <u>twists</u> the twigs into a small raft.				X	
1. Mark and Scott Kelly are <u>twins</u>.					
2. Scott <u>flies</u> combat planes.					
3. Mark and Scott <u>fly</u> into space.					
4. They are both <u>pilots</u>.					
5. Scott flew a <u>shuttle</u>.					
6. <u>Mark's</u> dream is to return to space.					
7. Elvis Presley had a <u>twin</u>.					
8. <u>Elvis'</u> twin did not live for very long.					
9. Kim and Kari Baker <u>live</u> in Libby, Montana.					
10. They work together with their <u>horses</u>.					

Exercise 2 · Verb or Noun

▶ Read these sentences.

▶ Circle "Noun" or "Verb" for the underlined word.

    1. He <u>dips</u> his hand into the damp sand.   Noun   or   Verb

    2. We had <u>dips</u> with our chips.   Noun   or   Verb

    3. Dan's asp did <u>tricks</u>.   Noun   or   Verb

    4. Dan <u>tricks</u> his twin.   Noun   or   Verb

    5. They hit their <u>backs</u> in the attic.   Noun   or   Verb

▶ Write two sentences for each of these words:

In the first sentence, use the word as a plural noun.

In the second sentence, use the word as a third person singular present tense verb.

    1. cracks: _____

         cracks: _____

    2. kicks: _____

         kicks: _____

    3. snacks: _____

         snacks: _____

    4. ticks: _____

         ticks: _____

    5. tracks: _____

         tracks: _____

Unit 4 · Lesson 7

Exercise 3 · Sentence Dictation

▸ Listen to each sentence.

▸ Repeat the sentence.

▸ Write it on the line.

▸ Underline the adverb or prepositional phrase in each sentence.

1. _____

2. _____

3. _____

4. _____

5. _____

▸ Using the adverbs or prepositional phrases you underlined:

1. Write the word or phrase that tells **when**: _____

2. Write the word or phrase that tells **how**: _____

3. Write the word or phrase that tells **where**: _____

_____

_____

▸ Rewrite sentences 1 and 4. Replace the subject with a pronoun.

_____

_____

Exercise 4 · Masterpiece Sentences: Stages 1 and 2

▸ Read the base sentence.

▸ Paint the predicate. Add a direct object, adverb, or prepositional phrase that acts as an adverb.

▸ Write your expanded sentence. Remember to use sentence signals at the beginning and end of the sentence.

1. The egg cracked. _____

_____

2. The twin picked. _____

_____

3. The wind twisted. _____

_____

4. The van skidded. _____

_____

5. Jack asked. _____

_____

Exercise 1 · Syllable Awareness

▶ Listen to the word.

▶ Say the word.

▶ Count and write the number of syllables.

▶ Write the letter for each vowel sound you hear.

	How many syllables do you hear?	First vowel sound	Second vowel sound	Third vowel sound
1.				
2.				
3.				
4.				
5.				
6.				
7.				
8.				
9.				
10.				

Exercise 2 · Sort It: Short / *a* / and Short / *i* /

▶ Sort the syllables in the **Syllable Bank** by vowel sound. Write the syllables in the appropriate column in the chart below.

Syllable Bank

nap	kid	vic	trans	tim
mit	ad	zig	can	zag
tic	at	rab	kin	did
tid				bit

▶ Build words using the syllables. Some syllables can be used more than once to build words. Write the words on the lines next to the chart.

short / *a* /	short / *i* /

_____

_____

_____

_____

_____

_____

_____

_____

_____

_____

Unit 4 · Lesson 8

Exercise 3 · Word Networks: Synonyms

▸ Write the synonym (same meaning) for the word your teacher says.

▸ Use the **Unit Vocabulary** list to find the synonym.

1. _____

2. _____

3. _____

4. _____

5. _____

Exercise 4 · Diagram It: Subject / Predicate With Adverbs

▸ Write the sentences from Lesson 7, exercise 3, in the diagrams.

1.
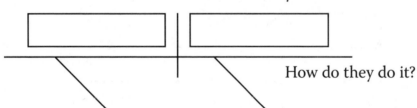

2.
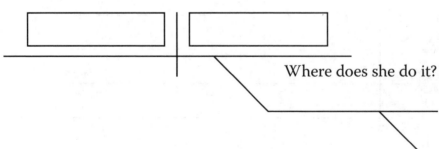

(continued)

Exercise 4 *(continued)* · **Diagram It: Subject/Predicate With Adverbs**

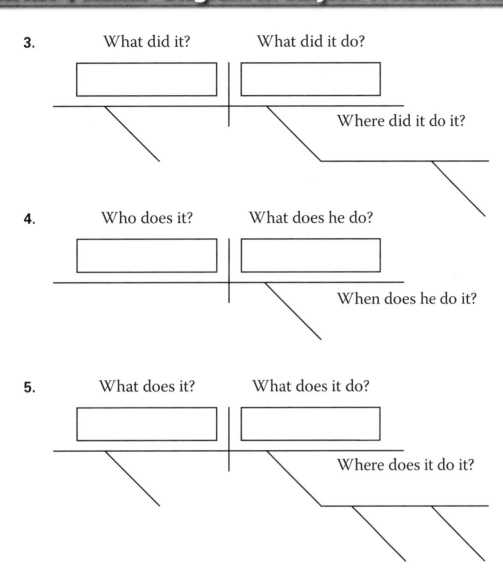

3. What did it?   What did it do?

Where did it do it?

4. Who does it?   What does he do?

When does he do it?

5. What does it?   What does it do?

Where does it do it?

Unit 4 · Lesson 8

Exercise 5 · Tense Timeline

▸ What signals the third person singular present tense verb form?

    ○ **-s** at the end   ○ **-ed** at the end   ○ **'s** at the end

▸ Write the three verbs that are third person singular present tense from the sentences in exercise 4.

_____

Exercise 6 · Reading Response: "Gemini: The Twins"

▸ Draw your own idea for a constellation of twins.

▸ Name the constellation.

▸ Share it with the class.

Exercise 1 · Syllable Awareness

▸ Listen to each word your teacher says.

▸ Repeat the word.

▸ Count the syllables.

▸ Write the letter for each vowel sound you hear.

	How many syllables do you hear?	First vowel sound	Second vowel sound
1.			
2.			
3.			
4.			
5.			
6.			
7.			
8.			
9.			
10.			

Exercise 2 · Listening for Word Parts

▸ Listen to each word.

▸ Write the part your teacher repeats.

1. _____   6. _____

2. _____   7. _____

3. _____   8. _____

4. _____   9. _____

5. _____   10. _____

Exercise 3 · Build It, Bank It

▸ Use the syllables from exercise 2 to build two-syllable words.

▸ Write them on the lines below.

_____

_____

_____

Unit 4 · Lesson 9

Exercise 4 · Sentence Dictation

▶ Listen to each sentence.

▶ Repeat the sentence.

▶ Write it on the line.

▶ Expand the predicate. Add:

- A direct object

- An adverb

- A prepositional phrase that acts as an adverb

1. _____

2. _____

3. _____

4. _____

5. _____

Exercise 1 • Listening for Sounds in Words

▸ Write the letters for the sounds you hear in each word.

▸ Circle the words your teacher says.

▸ Box the words your teacher says.

1.

2.

3.

4.

5.

6.

7.

8.

9.

10.

Check off the activities you complete with each lesson. Evaluate your accomplishments at the end of each lesson. Pay attention to teacher evaluations and comments.

Unit Objectives	Lesson 1 (Date:_____)	Lesson 2 (Date:_____)
STEP 1 **Phonemic Awareness and Phonics** • Say the sounds for consonants <u>l</u>, <u>f</u>, <u>z</u>, and <u>s</u>. • Write the letters for /l/, /f/, /z/, and /s/. • Say the sounds for vowel <u>o</u> (short /o/, /aw/). • Write the letter for short vowel sound /o/ and /aw/ as in **dog**. • Identify syllables in spoken words.	❑ Move It and Mark It ❑ Phonemic Drills ❑ See and Say ❑ Exercise 1: Say and Write ❑ Handwriting Practice	❑ Vowel Chart (T) ❑ Phonemic Drills ❑ See and Say ❑ Say and Write
STEP 2 **Word Recognition and Spelling** • Read and spell words with sound-spelling correspondences from this and previous units. • Read and spell the **Essential Words**: *here, there, these, why, those, where*.	❑ Exercise 2: Spelling Pretest ❑ Build It, Bank It ❑ Introduction: Double Consonants ❑ Memorize It	❑ Build It, Bank It ❑ Word Fluency 1 ❑ Memorize It ❑ Handwriting Practice
STEP 3 **Vocabulary and Morphology** • Define **Unit Vocabulary** words. • Form the progressive verb by adding the ending **-ing**, meaning ongoing action. • Identify word attributes: size, parts, color, function. • Define and use idioms.	❑ Unit Vocabulary ❑ Multiple Meaning Map (T)	❑ Introduction: Present Progressive Verb Ending ❑ Exercise 1: Find It ❑ Exercise 2: Rewrite It
STEP 4 **Grammar and Usage** • Identify present tense verbs. • Vary sentence structure by moving predicate painters within the sentence. • Use commas to set apart adverb phrases at the beginning of sentences.	❑ Review: Verbs ❑ Exercise 3: Code It	❑ Review: -s Endings ❑ Exercise 3: Identify It
STEP 5 **Listening and Reading** • Select topic and details from informational text. • Answer questions with **where** or **why**.	❑ Phrase Fluency 1 ❑ Exercise 4: Sentence Morphs	❑ Decodable Text: "What Is Jazz?" Mega-Dialog ❑ Sentence Fluency 1
STEP 6 **Speaking and Writing** • Expand base sentences with *when, where, how*. • Answer questions with **where** or **why**. • Record information on a graphic organizer.	❑ Masterpiece Sentences: Stages 1 and 2	❑ Masterpiece Sentences: Stages 1 and 2
Self-Evaluation (5 is the highest) **Effort** = I produced my best work. **Participation** = I was actively involved in tasks. **Independence** = I worked on my own.	**Effort:** 1 2 3 4 5 **Participation:** 1 2 3 4 5 **Independence:** 1 2 3 4 5	**Effort:** 1 2 3 4 5 **Participation:** 1 2 3 4 5 **Independence:** 1 2 3 4 5
Teacher Evaluation	**Effort:** 1 2 3 4 5 **Participation:** 1 2 3 4 5 **Independence:** 1 2 3 4 5	**Effort:** 1 2 3 4 5 **Participation:** 1 2 3 4 5 **Independence:** 1 2 3 4 5

Lesson 3 (Date:_____)	Lesson 4 (Date:_____)	Lesson 5 (Date:_____)
❑ Review: Consonants and Vowels (T) ❑ Phonemic Drills ❑ Exercise 1: Listening for Sounds in Words	❑ Review: Vowels and Consonants ❑ Phonemic Drills ❑ Exercise 1: Listening for Sounds in Words ❑ Letter-Sound Fluency	❑ Phonemic Drills ❑ Letter-Sound Fluency ❑ Exercise 1: Say and Write ❑ Content Mastery: Learning the Code
❑ Exercise 2: Listening for Word Parts ❑ Word Fluency 1 ❑ Exercise 3: Find It	❑ Chain It (T) ❑ Word Fluency 2 ❑ Type It ❑ Handwriting Practice	❑ Content Mastery: Spelling Posttest 1 ❑ Exercise 2: Sort It
❑ Exercise 4: Word Networks: Attributes ❑ Draw It	❑ More Present Progressive Verbs ❑ Exercise 2: Sort It ❑ Exercise 3: Rewrite It ❑ Exercise 4: Identify It	❑ Multiple Meaning Map (T)
❑ Review: Predicate Expansion ❑ Exercise 5: Diagram It	❑ More About Adverbs ❑ Masterpiece Sentences: Stage 3	❑ Exercise 3: Masterpiece Sentences: Stage 3
❑ Decodable Text: "What Is Jazz?" Mega-Dialog ❑ Instructional Text: "Jazz: The Recipe"	❑ Instructional Text: "Jazz: The Recipe" (T)	❑ Blueprint for Writing (T)
❑ Exercise 6: Answer It	❑ Blueprint for Writing (T) ❑ Challenge Text: "Growing Up With Jazz"	❑ Write It: A Paragraph (T) ❑ Challenge Text: "Growing Up With Jazz"
Effort: 1 2 3 4 5 **Participation:** 1 2 3 4 5 **Independence:** 1 2 3 4 5	**Effort:** 1 2 3 4 5 **Participation:** 1 2 3 4 5 **Independence:** 1 2 3 4 5	**Effort:** 1 2 3 4 5 **Participation:** 1 2 3 4 5 **Independence:** 1 2 3 4 5
Effort: 1 2 3 4 5 **Participation:** 1 2 3 4 5 **Independence:** 1 2 3 4 5	**Effort:** 1 2 3 4 5 **Participation:** 1 2 3 4 5 **Independence:** 1 2 3 4 5	**Effort:** 1 2 3 4 5 **Participation:** 1 2 3 4 5 **Independence:** 1 2 3 4 5

Check off the activities you complete with each lesson. Evaluate your accomplishments at the end of each lesson. Pay attention to teacher evaluations and comments.

Unit Objectives	Lesson 6 (Date:_____)	Lesson 7 (Date:_____)
STEP 1 **Phonemic Awareness and Phonics** • Say the sounds for consonants **l**, **f**, **z**, and **s**. • Write the letters for / l /, / f /, / z /, and / s /. • Say the sounds for vowel **o** (short / o /, / aw /). • Write the letter for short vowel sound / o / and / aw / as in **dog**. • Identify syllables in spoken words.	❏ Review: Consonants and Vowels ❏ Phonemic Drills ❏ Move It and Mark It ❏ Handwriting Practice	❏ Phonemic Drills ❏ See and Name ❏ Name and Write ❏ Listening for Sounds in Words ❏ Syllable Awareness
STEP 2 **Word Recognition and Spelling** • Read and spell words with sound-spelling correspondences from this and previous units. • Read and spell the **Essential Words:** *here, there, these, why, those, where.*	❏ Exercise 1: Spelling Pretest ❏ Exercise 2: Listening for Word Parts ❏ Exercise 3: Build It, Bank It ❏ Word Fluency 3	❏ Build It, Bank It
STEP 3 **Vocabulary and Morphology** • Define **Unit Vocabulary** words. • Form the progressive verb by adding the ending **-ing**, meaning ongoing action. • Identify word attributes: size, parts, color, function. • Define and use idioms.	❏ More About Compound Words ❏ Unit Vocabulary ❏ Exercise 4: Sort It	❏ Exercise 1: Rewrite It: From Plural to Singular ❏ Exercise 2: Rewrite It: From Present to Present Progressive ❏ Exercise 3: Find It
STEP 4 **Grammar and Usage** • Identify present tense verbs. • Vary sentence structure by moving predicate painters within the sentence. • Use commas to set apart adverb phrases at the beginning of sentences.	❏ Review: Moving the Predicate Painters ❏ Exercise 5: Masterpiece Sentences: Stage 3	❏ Tense Timeline ❏ Exercise 4: Choose It and Use It
STEP 5 **Listening and Reading** • Select topic and details from informational text. • Answer questions with **where** or **why**.	❏ Phrase Fluency 2 ❏ Exercise 6: Sentence Morphs	❏ Decodable Text: "What Is Jazz?" Mega-Dialog ❏ Sentence Fluency 2
STEP 6 **Speaking and Writing** • Expand base sentences with *when, where, how.* • Answer questions beginning with **where** or **why**. • Record information on a graphic organizer.	❏ Masterpiece Sentences: Stages 1, 2, and 3	❏ Sentence Types: Fact or Opinion
Self-Evaluation (5 is the highest) **Effort** = I produced my best work. **Participation** = I was actively involved in tasks. **Independence** = I worked on my own.	**Effort:** 1 2 3 4 5 **Participation:** 1 2 3 4 5 **Independence:** 1 2 3 4 5	**Effort:** 1 2 3 4 5 **Participation:** 1 2 3 4 5 **Independence:** 1 2 3 4 5
Teacher Evaluation	**Effort:** 1 2 3 4 5 **Participation:** 1 2 3 4 5 **Independence:** 1 2 3 4 5	**Effort:** 1 2 3 4 5 **Participation:** 1 2 3 4 5 **Independence:** 1 2 3 4 5

Lesson 8 (Date:_____)	Lesson 9 (Date:_____)	Lesson 10 (Date:_____)
❑ Phonemic Drills ❑ Letter-Name Fluency ❑ Exercise 1: Syllable Awareness	❑ Review: Vowel and Consonant Charts (T) ❑ Phonemic Drills ❑ Letter-Name Fluency ❑ Exercise 1: Syllable Awareness	❑ Exercise 1: Listening for Sounds in Words
❑ Review: Syllables ❑ Exercise 2: Sort It ❑ Word Fluency 4	❑ Chain It	❑ Content Mastery: Spelling Posttest 2
❑ Exercise 3: Word Networks: Attributes ❑ Content Mastery: Define It	❑ Multiple Meaning Map (T)	❑ Draw It ❑ Define It (T)
❑ Review: Present Progressive Verb Form ❑ Exercise 4: Sentence Dictation	❑ Exercise 2: Masterpiece Sentences: Stage 3	❑ Content Mastery: Nouns, Verbs, and Adverbs
❑ Decodable Text: "What Is Jazz?" Mega-Dialog ❑ Instructional Text: "Looking at Jazz"	❑ Exercise 3: Blueprint for Reading (T)	❑ Exercise 2: Blueprint for Reading (T)
❑ Exercise 5: Answer It	❑ Blueprint for Writing (T) ❑ Challenge Text: "The Duke Jazzes Newport"	❑ Blueprint for Writing (T) ❑ Challenge Text: "The Duke Jazzes Newport"
Effort: 1 2 3 4 5 **Participation:** 1 2 3 4 5 **Independence:** 1 2 3 4 5	**Effort:** 1 2 3 4 5 **Participation:** 1 2 3 4 5 **Independence:** 1 2 3 4 5	**Effort:** 1 2 3 4 5 **Participation:** 1 2 3 4 5 **Independence:** 1 2 3 4 5
Effort: 1 2 3 4 5 **Participation:** 1 2 3 4 5 **Independence:** 1 2 3 4 5	**Effort:** 1 2 3 4 5 **Participation:** 1 2 3 4 5 **Independence:** 1 2 3 4 5	**Effort:** 1 2 3 4 5 **Participation:** 1 2 3 4 5 **Independence:** 1 2 3 4 5

Lesson 1

Exercise 1 · Say and Write

▶ Write the letter or letters for each sound your teacher says.

▶ Say the sound as you write the letter or letters.

1. _____   3. _____   5. _____   7. _____   9. _____

2. _____   4. _____   6. _____   8. _____   10. _____

Exercise 2 · Spelling Pretest

▶ Write the words your teacher says.

1. _____   6. _____

2. _____   7. _____

3. _____   8. _____

4. _____   9. _____

5. _____   10. _____

Exercise 3 · Code It: Verbs

Part A:

▸ Read each sentence.

▸ Underline the predicate.

▸ Write a **V** over the verb in each sentence.

1. The critics pick jazz.

2. They give a gift.

3. The fans clap for the band.

4. Jazz impacts hip-hop today.

5. The past lives in jazz.

Part B:

1. Review sentences 1–5 above. Which two verbs are third person singular present tense form?

   _____

2. What ending signals this form of the present tense?

   _____

Exercise 4 · Sentence Morphs

▸ Practice scooping these phrases.

▸ Read them as you would speak them.

the critics pick jazz The critics pick jazz.	critics said it was strict Critics said it was strict.	the impact is fantastic The impact is fantastic.
the classics had an impact on rock. The classics had an impact on rock.	the past gives the strands The past gives the strands.	music from the past impacts jazz Music from the past impacts jazz.
picking crops was a hot job Picking crops was a hot job.	the facts are not valid The facts are not valid.	the cast had top hats The cast had top hats.

Exercise 1 • Find It: Present Progressive Verb Ending

▸ Listen as your teacher reads the sentences out loud.

▸ Underline each verb that ends with **-ing** and the word before it.

> **Example:**
>
> Inez <u>is digging</u> the jazz.

1. A bobcat is tracking Stan's cat.

2. Fidel is asking his dad for a laptop and a lapdog.

3. I am grilling hot dogs at the picnic.

4. They are crossing the pond on a raft.

5. The dog is sniffing the bobcat tracks.

6. Liz's plants are wilting on the sill.

7. Lin-Nam is jogging from the backstop.

8. Don and Jill are tossing rocks at a rotting log.

9. I am handing Rosa the limp plant.

10. Rosa is grilling the bass with yams.

Unit 5 · Lesson 2

Exercise 2 · Rewrite It: Present Progressive

▸ Read the verb in the first column.

▸ Add **-ing** to form the present progressive verb. Write the word in the second column.

▸ Read the verb phrases.

Verb	Present Progressive Form
1. rock	is _____
2. blast	is _____
3. print	am _____
4. cross	are _____
5. grasp	is _____
6. floss	am _____
7. drift	is _____
8. click	are _____
9. hiss	is _____
10. cost	is _____
11. mock	am _____
12. sniff	are _____

▸ Write three complete sentences using at least three of the present progressive verb phrases.

_____

_____

_____

_____

_____

Exercise 3 · Identify It: Noun or Verb

▸ Read each pair of sentences.

▸ Study each word with the -s ending.

▸ Is the -s word used as a noun or a verb? Make an X in the "Noun" or "Verb" column.

	Noun	Verb
1. She **blocks** him.		
She has six **blocks**.		
2. The ships stop at the **docks**.		
The ship **docks** here.		
3. Dad **grills** hot dogs.		
The **grills** were hot.		
4. He **spots** the asp in the grass.		
There are **spots** on that asp.		
5. We have trick **locks**.		
She **locks** the gift in the attic.		

Exercise 1 · Listening for Sounds in Words

▶ Put an X where you hear the short / *o* / sound.

1. ☐☐

2. ☐☐☐

3. ☐☐☐

4. ☐☐☐

5. ☐☐☐

Exercise 2 · Listening for Word Parts

▶ Listen to each word.

▶ Write the word part that your teacher repeats.

1. _____   6. _____

2. _____   7. _____

3. _____   8. _____

4. _____   9. _____

5. _____   10. _____

Exercise 3 · Find It: Essential Words

▸ Find the **Essential Words** for this unit in these sentences.

▸ Underline them. (There may be more than one in a sentence.)

1. Why are these jazz artists here?

2. We went there to sing.

3. These were classics.

4. Where are you playing jazz?

5. Music is playing here and there in New Orleans.

6. Here is where you play.

7. Those ingredients played a part in jazz.

▸ Write the **Essential Words** in the spaces.

▸ Circle the two **Essential Words** that rhyme.

_____   _____

_____   _____

_____   _____

Unit 5 · Lesson 3

Exercise 4 · Word Networks: Attributes

▸ Fill in the chart for these objects.

▸ Add additional objects your teacher selects, and write attributes for them.

Object	Size/Type	Parts	Color	Function
pen				
clock				
lock				
rock				

Exercise 5 · Diagram It: Subject/Predicate/Direct Object

▶ Read the sentences. Then fill in the diagrams.

1. Workers sang in the fields.

Who did it?   What did they do?

Where did they sing?

2. People sang songs at work.

Who did it?   What did they do?   Sang what?

Where did they sing them?

3. African Americans rewrote songs at church.

Who did it?   What did they do?   Rewrote what?

Where did they rewrite them?

(continued)

Exercise 5 (cont.) · **Diagram It: Subject/Predicate/Direct Object**

4. White Americans added ballads to jazz.

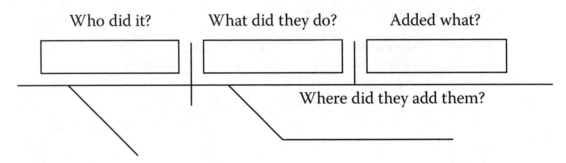

Who did it?   What did they do?   Added what?

Where did they add them?

5. Musicians played in dance halls.

Who did it?   What did they do?

Where did they play?

Exercise 6 · Answer It

▶ Answer each question in a complete sentence.

▶ Underline the part of the sentence that answers the question word.

1. Where did people sing work songs?

_____

_____

_____

2. What kind of music added to the recipe for jazz?

_____

_____

_____

3. What did African Americans do to change church music?

_____

_____

_____

4. What stories do ballads tell?

_____

_____

_____

5. Why were minstrel shows called variety shows?

_____

_____

_____

Exercise 1 · Listening for Sounds in Words

▸ Write the letter or letters for the sounds in the words your teacher says.

Example:

For the word **hop**, write:

h	o	p

▸ Circle the words that double the final consonants.

1. | | | |

2. | | |

3. | | | |

4. | | | |

5. | | | |

6. | | |

7. | | | |

8. | | | |

9. | | | |

10. | | | |

Exercise 2 · Sort It: Present and Present Progressive

▶ Read these phrases. Underline the main verb in each phrase.

▶ Write the phrase in the correct column according to the verb form.

▶ Read the phrase out loud after you write it to check your work.

> **Examples:**
>
> | Present Tense Verbs | Present Progressive Verbs |
> |---|---|
> | <u>lifts</u> the coffin | <u>is lifting</u> the coffin |
> | <u>spill</u> into the pond | <u>are spilling</u> into the pond |

1. stops the traffic

2. are stopping the traffic

3. is spilling the milk

4. spills the milk

5. are lifting it up

6. trips on a rock

7. drop the rock

8. are hissing at us

9. is mocking us

10. hops into the pond

Present Tense Verbs	Present Progressive Verbs

Unit 5 · Lesson 4

Exercise 3 · Rewrite It: Present Progressive

▸ Read the sentence in the first column. The underlined word is the present tense verb.

▸ Change the verb to the present progressive form. Write the new form of the verb in the blank in the second column.

▸ Read the sentence to check your answer.

Present Tense I rock, you rock, she rocks, we rock	Present Progressive Form I am rocking, you are rocking, she is rocking, we are rocking.
Examples: I sniff the grilled bass. The men lift the coffin.	**Examples:** I ___am sniffing___ the grilled bass. The men ___are lifting___ the coffin.
1. The cops block the traffic. **2.** I kick the rock off the dock. **3.** Scott rocks to the jazz. **4.** Lon-Ban plants the yams. **5.** The cat sniffs the catnip on the dock.	**1.** The cops _____ the traffic. **2.** I _____ the rock off the dock. **3.** Scott _____ to the jazz. **4.** Lon-Ban _____ the yams. **5.** The cat _____ the catnip on the dock.

Exercise 4 · Identify It: Present or Present Progressive

▸ Read each sentence.

▸ Look at the underlined verb.

▸ Decide if the underlined verb is in the present tense or present progressive form.

▸ Mark your choice by putting an X in the correct column.

	Present Tense	Present Progressive Form
Example: The twins <u>visit</u> the Hot Dog Grill.	X	
Example: Jack <u>kicks</u> the rocks off the dock.	X	
Example: The twins <u>are digging</u> the jazz.		X
1. Kim's boss <u>is stomping</u> on his laptop.		
2. That hot rod <u>is costing</u> me a lot.		
3. Scott's mom <u>is playing</u> jazz bass at the inn.		
4. Rosa and Hilda <u>fill</u> a bag of catnip for Hilda's manic cat, Clod.		
5. José <u>is clipping</u> a comic strip for me.		
6. We <u>flock</u> to the loft to play hot jazz.		
7. My mom <u>stops</u> at the grill to grab a snack.		
8. The cops <u>frisk</u> the bandits.		
9. Nick's dogs <u>are sniffing</u> Fran's wig.		
10. Tom <u>spills</u> the milk on Bill's livid duck.		

▸ Write the third person singular verbs here:

_____

Exercise 1 · Say and Write

▸ Write the letter for each sound your teacher says.

▸ Say the sound as you write the letter.

1. _____   3. _____   5. _____   7. _____   9. _____

2. _____   4. _____   6. _____   8. _____   10. _____

Exercise 2 · Sort It: Sounds for o

▸ Read the words in the box.

lost	blot	lot	boss	soft	sob	clog
clock	floss	flock	cross	cod	dog	dock

▸ Sort the words by the two sounds for **o**: short / o / and / aw /.

▸ Write the words in the correct vowel sound column.

short / o /	/ aw /

Exercise 3 · Masterpiece Sentences: Stage 3

▸ Underline the adverb or the prepositional phrase that acts like an adverb.

▸ Rewrite the sentence by moving the underlined part to the beginning.

▸ Does the underlined part of the sentence tell **how, when,** or **where?** Label it.

1. The plant wilts on the hot sill.

   _____

2. The cabin stands past the still pond.

   _____

3. Sal will hit the sack in a bit.

   _____

4. Scott drinks skim milk off and on.

   _____

5. Kim will act in the cast with skill.

   _____

Exercise 1 · Spelling Pretest

▸ Listen to each word.

▸ Write the words that your teacher repeats.

1. _____   6. _____

2. _____   7. _____

3. _____   8. _____

4. _____   9. _____

5. _____   10. _____

Exercise 2 · Listening for Word Parts

▸ Listen to each word.

▸ Write the word part that your teacher repeats.

1. _____   6. _____

2. _____   7. _____

3. _____   8. _____

4. _____   9. _____

5. _____   10. _____

Exercise 3 · Build It, Bank It

▸ Use the word parts in exercise 2 to build two-syllable words. Write them on the lines.

_____   _____   _____

_____   _____   _____

Exercise 4 · Sort It: Meaning Categories

▸ Read the words in the box.

jazz	brass	live	camping	golfing	rock
rafting	hip-hop	prom	twist	band	swimming

▸ Sort the words into the categories. (Some words may be used more than once.)

▸ Think of more words for each category.

Music	Dance	Activities

Exercise 5 · Masterpiece Sentences: Stage 3

▶ Read the base sentence.

▶ Add a predicate painter that answers **how, when,** or **where.**

▶ Move the predicate painter, and rewrite the sentence.

1. The band played _____ .
   (when)

   _____

   _____

2. The twins jog _____ .
   (where)

   _____

   _____

3. The clock ticks _____ .
   (how)

   _____

   _____

4. The fans clapped _____ .
   (when)

   _____

   _____

5. Jazz, rock, and hip-hop were classics _____ .
   (when)

   _____

   _____

Exercise 6 · Sentence Morphs

▸ Practice scooping these phrases. Read as you would speak them.

the past lives in jazz The past lives in jazz.	they kick to the music They kick to the music.	the backdrop is a sad past The backdrop is a sad past.
bands kick back and jam Bands kick back and jam.	jazz adds a new twist Jazz adds a new twist.	jazz has the fans and the music Jazz has the fans and the music.
the band had to sit still The band had to sit still.	the film was not fast The film was not fast.	the fabric of jazz is vivid The fabric of jazz is vivid.

Exercise 1 • Rewrite It: From Plural to Singular

▸ Listen to the sentence in the first column. Look at the underlined plural subject. Circle the verb.

▸ Listen to the sentence in the second column. Fill in the blank with the form of the verb that agrees with the singular subject.

Plural subject nouns Third person plural subjects, present tense verbs	Singular subject nouns Third person singular subjects, present tense verbs
Example: <u>They</u> (dig) jazz.	**Example:** She __digs__ jazz.
1. The <u>workers</u> sing at the dock.	1. The worker _____ at the dock.
2. <u>They</u> clap their hands to the beat of the music in church.	2. She _____ her hands to the beat of the music in church.
3. <u>They</u> tell sad stories in old, old songs.	3. He _____ sad stories in old, old songs.
4. The ragtime <u>tunes</u> fill the hall.	4. The ragtime tune _____ the hall.
5. <u>Jazz, blues, and ragtime</u> mimic the way we feel.	5. Jazz _____ the way we feel.

Exercise 2 · Rewrite It: From Present to Present Progressive

▸ Listen to the sentence in the first column. Underline the verb.

▸ Rewrite the sentence in the second column. Change the verb to present progressive form. Use **am, is,** or **are** with the **-ing** form of the verb.

Present Tense Happens now	Present Progressive Form (use **am, is,** or **are**) Ongoing action happening right now
Example: The flappers <u>rock</u> to the music.	**Example:** The flappers are rocking to the music.
1. People buzz about the hot new jazz trumpet player.	1.
2. Don stands by his slick red car.	2.
3. He helps the flapper into his hot rod.	3.
4. The flapper and Don rock to the music.	4.
5. The jazz ends.	5.

Exercise 3 · Find It: Present Progressive

▸ Listen as your teacher reads the passage out loud.

▸ Identify the verb in each sentence.

▸ Underline the verbs that are in the present progressive form.

Frogs are fond of ponds. A mob of them is hopping from the grass into the pond. They are swimming. The frogs swim to the land and hop on the sand. Some frogs are basking on the dock. Some frogs are sitting on a rock. Some frogs are plopping on the damp moss. They trill in the soft grass.

A swift dog is running into the soft grass. It sniffs the grass. It is tracking frogs. Dogs are fond of tracking frogs. The frogs are panicking. They are hopping fast to the pond. They are spilling back into the pond. The tracking dog is gone.

Unit 5 · Lesson 7

Exercise 4 · Choose It and Use It

Part A: Noun-Verb Agreement

▶ Listen to the sentence.

▶ Circle the correct form of the verb to agree with the subject noun or pronoun.

▶ Write the word in the blank.

▶ Read the sentence to check.

    1. He _____ in the field. (sing or sings)

    2. She _____ at work. (hum or hums)

    3. They _____ the beat of the jazz. (change or changes)

    4. The ballad _____ a story. (tell or tells)

    5. Ragtime songs _____ the dance hall walls. (rock or rocks)

▶ List the third person singular present tense verbs used in these sentences.

_____

Part B: Present or Present Progressive Verb Form

▶ Listen to the sentences.

▶ Circle the correct form of the present tense verb for each sentence.

▶ Write the word in the blank.

▶ Read the sentence to check.

    1. She is _____ to the music. (stomps or stomping)

    2. The band _____ with the beat of the jazz. (rocks or rocking)

    3. They are _____ the beat. (change or changing)

    4. The ballad is _____ a sad story. (tells or telling)

    5. The fans are _____ to the beat of the song. (clap or clapping)

▶ List the present progressive verb forms used in these sentences.

_____

Exercise 1 · Syllable Awareness

▸ Listen to the word your teacher says.

▸ Count the syllables.

▸ Write the letter for each vowel sound you hear.

	How many syllables do you hear?	First vowel sound	Second vowel sound	Third vowel sound
1.				
2.				
3.				
4.				
5.				
6.				
7.				
8.				
9.				

Unit 5 · Lesson 8

Exercise 2 · Sort It: Vowel Sounds

▶ Read the words in the **Syllable Bank**.

▶ Sort the syllables in the **Syllable Bank** by vowel sound. Write the syllables in the table below.

Syllable Bank

as	cross	can	ic	wind
not	back	rap	pop	off
id	mim	prof	hot	non
mill	cot	criss	log	tag
dog	top	it	tip	fat

▶ Build two-syllable words using the syllables. Some syllables can be used more than once to build words.

▶ Write the words at the bottom of the table.

short / *a* /	short / *i* /	short / *o* /	/ *aw* /

Two-syllable words: _____

_____

Exercise 3 · Word Networks: Attributes

▸ Read the words in the **Word Bank**.

Word Bank

blond	damp	plastic	soft	fast
last	black	odd	flat	hot

▸ Listen to the sentence.

▸ Fill in the blank with a word from the **Word Bank**. More than one word may apply.

1. She wore a _____ wig.

2. They looked at the _____ map on the table.

3. He took the _____ pot from the stove.

4. She got the _____ job she wanted.

5. A _____ mask was part of the bat costume.

6. He wiped the cab with a _____ rag.

7. The shop put the pot in a _____ bag.

8. The _____ rabbit was a gift.

9. The _____ cab got to the airport in time.

10. At the end of the concert, they sang the _____ song.

Exercise 4 · Sentence Dictation

▶ Listen to each sentence.

▶ Repeat the sentence.

▶ Write it on the numbered line.

▶ Expand the predicate by adding **one** of the following to each sentence:

• A direct object

• An adverb

• A prepositional phrase that acts as an adverb

▶ Write the expanded sentence on the line below the original sentence.

▶ Underline the present progressive form of the verb in each sentence.

> **Example:**
> They <u>are planning</u> a party.
> (**party** is a direct object)

1. _____

   _____

2. _____

   _____

3. _____

   _____

4. _____

   _____

5. _____

   _____

Exercise 5 · Answer It

▶ Answer these questions. Underline the part of the sentence that replaces the question word. For example, underline the reason or explanation in answers to "why" questions.

1. What do pictures of jazz show?

_____

_____

2. When was the Jazz Age?

_____

_____

3. Why did artists use strange lines and unusual colors?

_____

_____

4. How does music inspire art?

_____

_____

5. Why did artists take or draw jazz pictures?

_____

_____

Lesson 9

Exercise 1 · Syllable Awareness

▸ Listen to the word your teacher says.

▸ Count the syllables.

▸ Write the letter for each vowel sound you hear.

	How many syllables do you hear?	First vowel sound	Second vowel sound	Third vowel sound
1.				
2.				
3.				
4.				
5.				
6.				
7.				
8.				
9.				
10.				

Exercise 2 · Masterpiece Sentences: Stage 3

▶ Answer the questions.

▶ Combine the answers to write a sentence.

▶ Use the *Student Text,* pages 169–171, **"Looking at Jazz"** for information to answer the questions.

1. Who did it?   **flappers**

What did they do?   _____

When did they do it?   _____

_____

2. Who did it?   **painters**

What did they do?   _____

How did they do it?   _____

_____

3. Who did it?   **photographers**

What did they do?   _____

When did they do it?   _____

_____

4. Who did it?   **artists**

What did they do?   _____

How did they do it?   _____

_____

5. Who did it?   **people**

What did they do?   _____

Where did they do it?   _____

_____

(continued)

Exercise 2 (continued) · Masterpiece Sentences: Stage 3

▶ Rewrite **two** of your sentences. Move the predicate painters to change the structure.

_____

_____

_____

_____

▶ Diagram **two** of your sentences.

Exercise 3 · Blueprint for Reading

▸ Highlight the main ideas in blue and the details in pink in the text.

from "Looking at Jazz"

We *hear* jazz. But can we *see* it? Some have tried. Artists have captured jazz. The music is alive. Some can catch its spirit. They show people. They show them playing. They show them dancing. They use color. They use line. They *show* jazz. They show the **mood**. They show the feeling.

It was the Jazz Age. Go back to the 1920s. Jazz was *it*. It was like rock and rap today. Kids loved it. It was more than popular. It was the *in thing*. The '20s were new. They were special. How? People felt alive. They felt free. They had fun. Jazz! Flappers! What were flappers? They were young women. They loved jazz. They loved dancing to jazz. Artists loved to paint them dancing.

Exercise 1 · Listening for Sounds in Words

▶ Write the letter or letters in each box for the sounds in the words your teacher says.

Example:

For the word **hop**, write: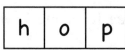

▶ In words 1–5, circle the words with / *l* / at the end.

▶ In words 6–10, circle the word that rhymes with **fog**.

▶ In words 6–10, put a box around the word that rhymes with **cost**.

1. ☐☐☐

2. ☐☐☐

3. ☐☐☐

4. ☐☐☐

5. ☐☐☐

6. ☐☐☐☐

7. ☐☐☐☐

8. ☐☐☐☐

9. ☐☐☐☐

10. ☐☐☐☐

Exercise 2 · Blueprint for Reading

▸ Highlight the main ideas in blue and the details in pink in the text.

from "Looking at Jazz"

Sometimes, artists changed things. They changed what they saw. They changed the look of things. They used strange lines. They used **bold** colors. The colors made moods. They used different lines. Curved lines are restful. Zigzag lines are nervous. Black is gloomy. Red is exciting. Artists changed the colors. They changed the scenes. They got the mood. They got the feeling. They painted jazz.

Music **inspires** art. You can spot these pictures. They *look* like jazz. They look like the music. They have **rhythm**. They have color. They have strong lines.

Photographers captured jazz, too. Photography got better. First, film was faster. Then, flash became portable. This was important. Photographers could work at the shows. They could take pictures of jazz. They'd find the right angle. They'd wait for the right moment. Then, they'd snap!

Artists have caught the jazz feeling. Jazz can be pictures. They are loud. They are strong. They are lively. They are **distinct**. They are like the music. They *are* jazz!

Check off the activities you complete with each lesson. Evaluate your accomplishments at the end of each lesson. Pay attention to teacher evaluations and comments.

Unit Objectives	Lesson 1 (Date:_____)	Lesson 2 (Date:_____)
STEP 1 **Phonemic Awareness and Phonics** • Say the sounds for the consonants <u>x</u> and <u>qu</u>. • Write the letters for the sounds / ks / and / kw /. • Identify syllables in spoken words.	❏ Move It and Mark It ❏ Phonemic Drills ❏ See and Say ❏ Exercise 1: Say and Write ❏ Handwriting Practice	❏ Vowel Chart (T) ❏ Phonemic Drills ❏ See and Say ❏ Say and Write
STEP 2 **Word Recognition and Spelling** • Read and spell words with sound-spelling correspondences from this and previous units. • Read and spell the **Essential Words:** *how, now, down, her, me, for.* • Spell words using the **Doubling Rule.**	❏ Exercise 2: Spelling Pretest ❏ Build It, Bank It ❏ Memorize It	❏ Build It, Bank It ❏ Word Fluency 1 ❏ Memorize It ❏ Handwriting Practice
STEP 3 **Vocabulary and Morphology** • Define **Unit Vocabulary** words. • Review present tense and present progressive verb forms. • Classify **Unit Vocabulary** words by attributes.	❏ Unit Vocabulary ❏ Multiple Meaning Map (T)	❏ Exercise 1: Review: Present Tense Verbs ❏ Exercise 2: Review: Present Progressive Verbs ❏ Exercise 3: Rewrite It
STEP 4 **Grammar and Usage** • Replace nouns with pronouns (nominative, objective). • Identify prepositions and prepositional phrases. • Identify adjectives that tell *which one, how many,* or *what kind.*	❏ Review: Pronouns ❏ Exercise 3: Rewrite It: Pronouns	❏ Introduction: Objective Pronouns ❏ Exercise 4: Rewrite It: Pronouns
STEP 5 **Listening and Reading** • Read with inflection, phrasing, and expression. • Answer questions with **how.** • Select the topic and details from informational text.	❏ Phrase Fluency ❏ Exercise 4: Sentence Morphs	❏ Decodable Text: "Toxic Pollutants" Mega-Dialog ❏ Sentence Fluency
STEP 6 **Speaking and Writing** • Generate sentences using **Unit Vocabulary.** • Expand the base sentence with *when, where,* or *how.* • Write answers to questions with **who, what, when, where,** or **how.** • Record information on a graphic organizer.	❏ Review: Masterpiece Sentences: Stages 1 and 2	❏ Masterpiece Sentences: Stages 1 and 2

Self-Evaluation (5 is the highest)
  Effort = I produced my best work.
  Participation = I was actively involved in tasks.
  Independence = I worked on my own.
	Effort: 1 2 3 4 5
	Participation: 1 2 3 4 5
	Independence: 1 2 3 4 5
		Effort: 1 2 3 4 5
		Participation: 1 2 3 4 5
		Independence: 1 2 3 4 5

Teacher Evaluation	**Effort:** 1 2 3 4 5 **Participation:** 1 2 3 4 5 **Independence:** 1 2 3 4 5	**Effort:** 1 2 3 4 5 **Participation:** 1 2 3 4 5 **Independence:** 1 2 3 4 5

Lesson 3 (Date:_____)	**Lesson 4** (Date:_____)	**Lesson 5** (Date:_____)
❏ Review: Consonant and Vowel Charts ❏ Phonemic Drills ❏ Exercise 1: Listening for Sounds in Words	❏ Review: Vowels and Consonants ❏ Phonemic Drills ❏ Exercise 1: Listening for Sounds in Words ❏ Letter-Sound Fluency	❏ Phonemic Drills ❏ Letter-Sound Fluency ❏ Exercise 1: Say and Write
❏ Exercise 2: Listening for Word Parts ❏ Review: Double Consonants ❏ Word Fluency 1 ❏ Exercise 3: Find It	❏ Chain It ❏ Introduction: Doubling Rule ❏ Double It (T) ❏ Word Fluency 2 ❏ Type It ❏ Handwriting Practice	❏ Exercise 2: Sort It ❏ Content Mastery: Spelling Posttest 1
❏ Exercise 4: Word Networks: Antonyms ❏ Exercise 5: Define It	❏ Exercise 2: Rewrite It: From Present to Present Progressive ❏ Morphology Recap ❏ Exercise 3: Identify It	❏ Multiple Meaning Map (T)
❏ More About Prepositions (T) ❏ Exercise 6: Find It	❏ Preposition Practice (T) ❏ Introduction: Adjectives ❏ Exercise 4: Sort It	❏ Preposition Practice (T) ❏ More About Adjectives ❏ Masterpiece Sentences: Stage 4
❏ Decodable Text: "Toxic Pollutants" Mega-Dialog ❏ Instructional Text: "Rachel Carson"	❏ Instructional Text: "Rachel Carson" (T)	❏ Instructional Text: "Rachel Carson" (T)
❏ Exercise 7: Answer It	❏ Blueprint for Writing (T) ❏ Challenge Text: "Riddle of the Frogs"	❏ Write It: A Paragraph ❏ Challenge Text: "Riddle of the Frogs"
Effort: 1 2 3 4 5 **Participation:** 1 2 3 4 5 **Independence:** 1 2 3 4 5	**Effort:** 1 2 3 4 5 **Participation:** 1 2 3 4 5 **Independence:** 1 2 3 4 5	**Effort:** 1 2 3 4 5 **Participation:** 1 2 3 4 5 **Independence:** 1 2 3 4 5
Effort: 1 2 3 4 5 **Participation:** 1 2 3 4 5 **Independence:** 1 2 3 4 5	**Effort:** 1 2 3 4 5 **Participation:** 1 2 3 4 5 **Independence:** 1 2 3 4 5	**Effort:** 1 2 3 4 5 **Participation:** 1 2 3 4 5 **Independence:** 1 2 3 4 5

Lesson Checklist
Lessons 6–7

Check off the activities you complete with each lesson. Evaluate your accomplishments at the end of each lesson. Pay attention to teacher evaluations and comments.

Unit Objectives	Lesson 6 (Date:_____)	Lesson 7 (Date:_____)
STEP 1 **Phonemic Awareness and Phonics** • Say the sounds for the consonants <u>x</u> and <u>qu</u>. • Write the letters for the sounds / ks / and / kw /. • Identify syllables in spoken words.	❑ Review: Consonants and Vowels ❑ Phonemic Drills ❑ Exercise 1: Listening for Sounds in Words ❑ Handwriting Practice	❑ Phonemic Drills ❑ See and Name ❑ Name and Write ❑ Listening for Sounds in Words ❑ Syllable Awareness
STEP 2 **Word Recognition and Spelling** • Read and spell words with sound-spelling correspondences from this and previous units. • Read and spell the **Essential Words:** *how, now, down, her, me, for.* • Spell words using the **Doubling Rule.**	❑ Exercise 2: Spelling Pretest ❑ Exercise 3: Build It, Bank It ❑ Word Fluency 3	❑ Exercise 1: Review: Doubling Rule ❑ Double It (T)
STEP 3 **Vocabulary and Morphology** • Define **Unit Vocabulary** words. • Review present tense and present progressive verb forms. • Classify **Unit Vocabulary** words by attributes.	❑ Review: Vocabulary ❑ Exercise 4: Classify It	❑ Exercise 2: Find It ❑ Exercise 3: Rewrite It ❑ Exercise 4: More Find It
STEP 4 **Grammar and Usage** • Replace nouns with pronouns (nominative, objective). • Identify prepositions and prepositional phrases. • Identify adjectives that tell *which one, how many,* or *what kind.*	❑ Preposition Practice (T) ❑ Subject Expansion ❑ Exercise 5: Code It ❑ Exercise 6: Diagram It 1 and 2	❑ Preposition Practice ❑ Exercise 5: Sentence Dictation
STEP 5 **Listening and Reading** • Read with inflection, phrasing, and expression. • Answer questions with **how.** • Select the topic and details from informational text.	❑ Instructional Text: "Coming Clean About Toxic Pollution"	❑ Exercise 6: Blueprint for Reading
STEP 6 **Speaking and Writing** • Generate sentences using **Unit Vocabulary.** • Expand the base sentence with *when, where,* or *how.* • Write answers to questions with **who, what, when, where,** or **how.** • Record information on a graphic organizer.	❑ Exercise 7: Answer It	❑ Exercise 7: Blueprint for Writing (T) ❑ Challenge Text: "Amazon Toxins"
Self-Evaluation (5 is the highest) **Effort** = I produced my best work. **Participation** = I was actively involved in tasks. **Independence** = I worked on my own.	**Effort:** 1 2 3 4 5 **Participation:** 1 2 3 4 5 **Independence:** 1 2 3 4 5	**Effort:** 1 2 3 4 5 **Participation:** 1 2 3 4 5 **Independence:** 1 2 3 4 5
Teacher Evaluation	**Effort:** 1 2 3 4 5 **Participation:** 1 2 3 4 5 **Independence:** 1 2 3 4 5	**Effort:** 1 2 3 4 5 **Participation:** 1 2 3 4 5 **Independence:** 1 2 3 4 5

Lesson 8 (Date:_____)	Lesson 9 (Date:_____)	Lesson 10 (Date:_____)
❏ Phonemic Drills ❏ Letter-Name Fluency ❏ Exercise 1: Syllable Awareness	❏ Review: Vowel and Consonant Charts (T) ❏ Phonemic Drills ❏ Letter-Name Fluency ❏ Syllable Awareness ❏ Exercise 1: Listening for Sounds in Words	❏ Summative Test: Phonemic Awareness and Phonics
❏ Exercise 2: Listening for Word Parts ❏ Word Fluency 4 ❏ Progress Indicators: TOSWRF	❏ Progress Indicators: Spelling Inventory	❏ Content Mastery: Spelling Posttest 2
❏ Exercise 3: Word Networks: Antonyms, Synonyms, and Attributes		❏ Summative Test: Vocabulary and Morphology
❏ Exercise 4: Diagram It 1 and 2	❏ Review: Adjectives ❏ Masterpiece Sentences: Stages 1, 2, and 4 ❏ Exercise 2: Sort It	❏ Summative Test: Grammar and Usage
❏ Exercise 5: Blueprint for Reading		❏ Progress Indicators: Degrees of Reading Power (DRP)
❏ Exercise 6: Blueprint for Writing (T) ❏ Challenge Text: "Amazon Toxins"	❏ Summative Test: Composition	
Effort: 1 2 3 4 5 **Participation:** 1 2 3 4 5 **Independence:** 1 2 3 4 5	**Effort:** 1 2 3 4 5 **Participation:** 1 2 3 4 5 **Independence:** 1 2 3 4 5	**Effort:** 1 2 3 4 5 **Participation:** 1 2 3 4 5 **Independence:** 1 2 3 4 5
Effort: 1 2 3 4 5 **Participation:** 1 2 3 4 5 **Independence:** 1 2 3 4 5	**Effort:** 1 2 3 4 5 **Participation:** 1 2 3 4 5 **Independence:** 1 2 3 4 5	**Effort:** 1 2 3 4 5 **Participation:** 1 2 3 4 5 **Independence:** 1 2 3 4 5

Exercise 1 · Say and Write

▶ Write the letter or letters for each sound your teacher says.

▶ Say the sound as you write the letter or letters.

1. _____   3. _____   5. _____   7. _____   9. _____

2. _____   4. _____   6. _____   8. _____   10. _____

Exercise 2 · Spelling Pretest

▶ Listen to the words your teacher says.

▶ Write the words your teacher repeats.

1. _____   6. _____

2. _____   7. _____

3. _____   8. _____

4. _____   9. _____

5. _____   10. _____

Exercise 3 · Rewrite It: Pronouns

▸ In the sentences below, underline the noun that is the subject of the sentence.

▸ Change the subject *noun* to a *pronoun*. (Use the pronouns in the box below.)

I	we
you	you
he	they
she	
it	

▸ Write the new sentence on the line.

▸ Circle the pronoun that is the new subject of the sentence.

1. The fox left tracks in the sand.

_____

2. The milkman is quitting at six.

_____

3. The frogs are hopping in the pond.

_____

4. My boss and I discuss how to fix the toxins.

_____

5. The wax is spilling on the quilt.

_____

Exercise 4 · Sentence Morphs

▸ Practice scooping these phrases.

▸ Read as you would speak them.

• we could • • spot bass and frogs • We could spot bass and frogs.	• the plot of land • • was vast • The plot of land was vast.	• the facts • • prompt me to act • The facts prompt me to act.
• the cost • • to the land • • is vast • The cost to the land is vast.	• the task • • is to stop toxins • The task is to stop toxins.	• toxic pollution • • is bad • Toxic pollution is bad.
• I had to • • give the facts • I had to give the facts.	• they said • • toxins can kill • They said toxins can kill.	• I had plans • • to fix • • the impact of DDT • I had plans to fix the impact of DDT.

Exercise 1 · Review: Present Tense Verbs

▶ Read the verb.

▶ Read the sentence and circle the subject. Is the subject a singular noun or third person singular pronoun (he, she, or it)?

▶ Write the verb in the blank. Add **-s** to match the subject if necessary.

Verb	Present Tense Sentence
Examples: stop blab	(He)_____**stops**_____ the van. (They)_____**blab**_____ when they sit on the dock.
1. quit	**1.** He _____ his job at the dock.
2. quack	**2.** The black ducks _____ on the pond.
3. spot	**3.** He _____ the raft drifting on the pond.
4. profit	**4.** The inn _____ from our jazz band.
5. limit	**5.** They _____ Jim's visits to the pond.
6. flop	**6.** The frog _____ on the plot of grass.
7. hand	**7.** She _____ me the toxic black frogs.
8. plan	**8.** The cast _____ a picnic for Max.
9. zigzag	**9.** The lost dog _____ across the pond.
10. visit	**10.** We _____ Rob in his cabin on top of the hill.

Unit 6 · Lesson 2

Exercise 2 · Review: Present Progressive Verbs

▶ Listen as your teacher reads the sentences out loud.

▶ Select a response from the box to fill in the blanks.

▶ Write the word in the blank.

-ing	now	are
is	am	

1. We add the suffix _____ to a verb to make the progressive form.

2. We use _____, _____ , or _____ with the progressive form of the verb to make it present.

3. The present progressive shows us the action is happening right _____. The action is ongoing.

Exercise 3 · Rewrite It: Present Progressive

▸ Read the verb in the first column.

▸ Add **-ing** and write the verb in the blank in the second column.

▸ Read the present progressive verb phrase.

Verb	Present Progressive Phrase
Examples: miss flick	is _____missing_____ are _____flicking_____
1. quack	**1.** are _____
2. quilt	**2.** am _____
3. boss	**3.** are _____
4. hiss	**4.** is _____
5. stock	**5.** are _____

Unit 6 · Lesson 2

Exercise 4 · Rewrite It: Pronouns

▶ Review the **objective pronouns** in the box.

me	us
you	you
him, her, it	them

▶ Rewrite each sentence, replacing the underlined word with an objective pronoun.

▶ Fill in a bubble to show if the pronoun is:

- a direct object or

- an object of a preposition.

Example:

Sal gives gifts to <u>victims</u>.

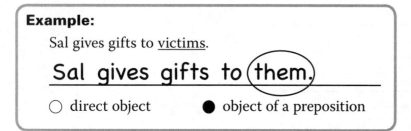

Sal gives gifts to (them.)

○ direct object   ● object of a preposition

1. The fox left <u>tracks</u> in the sand.

_____

○ direct object   ○ object of a preposition

2. Toxins are dripping into the <u>sand</u>.

_____

○ direct object   ○ object of a preposition

3. The scientist digs the <u>plants</u> in the lab.

_____

○ direct object   ○ object of a preposition

(continued)

Exercise 4 (continued) · Rewrite It: Pronouns

4. The toxic gas kills the <u>crops</u>.

_____

    ○ direct object   ○ object of a preposition

5. The wax is dripping on the <u>quilt</u>.

_____

    ○ direct object   ○ object of a preposition

Exercise 1 · Listening for Sounds in Words

▸ Put an X where you hear the / *k* / sound in the words your teacher says.

▸ If you do not hear / *k* /, write the sounds for the word in the boxes.

1. ▢▢▢

2. ▢▢▢

3. ▢▢▢

4. ▢▢▢

5. ▢▢▢▢

6. ▢▢▢▢

7. ▢▢▢▢

8. ▢▢▢▢

9. ▢▢▢▢

10. ▢▢▢▢

Exercise 2 · Listening for Word Parts

▸ Listen to each word.

▸ Write the word part your teacher repeats.

1. _____   6. _____

2. _____   7. _____

3. _____   8. _____

4. _____   9. _____

5. _____   10. _____

Exercise 3 · Find It: Essential Words

▸ Find the Unit 6 **Essential Words** in these sentences.

▸ Underline those words. There may be more than one in a sentence.

1. Give me the box.

2. Can you fix it for me?

3. She got the fax for her boss.

4. How will you do that?

5. The quints slid down the hill.

6. Gram has down quilts on her cots.

7. Quinn has it for me now.

▸ Write the **Essential Words** in the spaces.

▸ Circle the two **Essential Words** that rhyme.

_____   _____

_____   _____

_____   _____

Exercise 4 · Word Networks: Antonyms

▶ Read the words in the box. Select the antonym, or opposite, for the word your teacher says.

off	down	toxic	fix	top
quit	now	from	there	quick

1. _____

2. _____

3. _____

4. _____

5. _____

6. _____

7. _____

8. _____

9. _____

10. _____

Exercise 5 · Define It

Category   Attributes

1. fix **=**

               +

Definition: _____

_____

Category   Attributes

2. quilt **=**

               +

Definition: _____

_____

Category   Attributes

3. quiz **=**

               +

Definition: _____

_____

Unit 6 · Lesson 3

Exercise 6 · Find It: Prepositions

▶ Listen and follow along as your teacher reads these sentences.

▶ Underline the preposition in each sentence.

▶ Put an X in the correct column to indicate if the preposition shows:

- Position in *space* or

- Position in *time*.

	Space	Time
1. The toxins spill into the still pond.		
2. The asp slid under the flat rock.		
3. During the contest, the fans were clapping.		
4. From the cabin, the man spotted a bobcat.		
5. The crab left tracks on the damp sand.		
6. The boss was here until 6:00 p.m.		
7. A toxic mist is dropping over the vast crops.		
8. The frogs are hopping near the pond.		
9. The van was zigzagging across the traffic.		
10. Since the big win, the tennis fans are very happy.		

▶ Write the prepositions from the sentences on the line below.

▶ Circle the prepositions that signal *time*.

_____

_____

Exercise 7 · Answer It

▸ Underline the part of the answer that replaces the question word. For example, underline the way something is done or happens in "how" questions.

1. Who is Rachel Carson?

_____

_____

_____

2. What is DDT?

_____

_____

_____

3. How are pesticides helpful?

_____

_____

_____

How are they harmful?

_____

_____

_____

Exercise 1 · Listening for Sounds in Words

▶ Read each word.

▶ Fill in the chart with the number of letters and sounds in each word.

	How many letters are in the word?	How many sounds are in the word?
1. fox		
2. fog		
3. box		
4. boss		
5. quints		
6. mix		
7. quilt		
8. quiz		
9. wax		
10. quit		

Exercise 2 · Rewrite It: From Present to Present Progressive

▸ Listen to the sentence in the first column. Underline the verb.

▸ Complete the sentence in the second column by changing the verb to present progressive form. Use **am**, **is**, or **are** with the **-ing** verb form.

▸ Remember to use the **Doubling Rule** when needed.

Present Tense Happens now	Present Progressive Ongoing action happening right now
Examples: Kim <u>drops</u> the cod into the hot pot. Toxins <u>deform</u> the legs of frogs.	Kim ___*is dropping*___ the cod into the hot pot. Toxins *are deforming* the legs of frogs.
1. Rosa stops traffic to let the fox cross the ramp.	1. Rosa _____ traffic to let the fox cross the ramp.
2. I dig Max's classic comics.	2. I _____ Max's classic comics.
3. Lin grabs the silk napkins from the hatbox.	3. Lin _____ the silk napkins from the hatbox.
4. I hand the socks to Fidel's mom.	4. I _____ the socks to Fidel's mom.
5. Ron's dad quits his toxic habits.	5. Ron's dad _____ his toxic habits.

Unit 6 · Lesson 4

Exercise 3 · Identify It: Noun and Verb Forms

Morphology Recap

▸ Use the suffix **-s** to:

  • Form a plural noun (two or more).

  • Form the third person singular present tense verb (she **zips**).

▸ Use the suffix **'s** to:

  • Form a singular possessive noun (the owner).

▸ Use the suffix **-ing** and **am**, **is**, or **are** to:

  • Form the present progressive verb.

▸ Read each sentence in the first column of the table on the next page.

▸ Look at the underlined word or words in each sentence.

▸ Look at the columns. Mark the choice that identifies the form of the underlined words.

▸ Write the third person singular present tense verbs on the line below the table.

	Nouns			Verbs	
	Singular	Singular possessive	Plural	Third person singular present tense	Present progressive
Example: Kim <u>is stopping</u> the toxic spills in the pond.					X
Example: Don spills water on <u>Kim's</u> deformed frog.		X			

(continued)

Exercise 3 (continued) · Identify It: Noun and Verb Forms

	Nouns			Verbs	
	Singular	Singular possessive	Plural	Third person singular present tense	Present progressive
1. Kim grabs a deformed <u>frog</u> from the pond.					
2. The frog <u>flops</u> like a fish on land.					
3. Don <u>is swimming</u> from the raft to the dock.					
4. He spots frogs flopping like <u>Kim's</u> frog.					
5. Don and Kim take a deformed frog to the <u>cops</u>.					
6. The cops quiz Kim and Don about the deformed <u>frog</u>.					
7. Kim <u>is telling</u> the cops where the frog was in the pond.					
8. The cops track down the hill and across <u>rocks</u> to the pond.					
9. Kim <u>sniffs</u> toxic gas in the grass by the dock.					
10. The <u>pond's</u> water was toxic from gas dripping from the pump on the dock.					

Exercise 4 · Sort It: Which One? How Many? What Kind?

▸ Listen to each sentence and review the underlined adjective word or phrase.

▸ Write the underlined words and phrases in the correct column in the template.

1. The <u>hot</u> wax is dripping on the mat.

2. The <u>brisk</u> air was polluted.

3. <u>That</u> bobcat hid in the cabin.

4. The cab <u>with the flat</u> stopped traffic.

5. <u>Six</u> frogs were in the lab.

6. The crabs were digging into the <u>damp</u> sand.

7. <u>Many</u> toxins pollute the air.

8. Gas mist <u>from vans and cabs</u> clogs the environment.

9. The <u>vivid</u> quilt was a gift for her.

10. The <u>toxic</u> plant made them sick.

Which one?	How many?	What kind?

Exercise 1 · Say and Write

▸ Write the letter or letters for each sound your teacher says.

▸ Say the sound as you write the letter or letters.

1. _____   3. _____   5. _____   7. _____   9. _____

2. _____   4. _____   6. _____   8. _____   10. _____

Exercise 2 · Sort It: Common Sounds

▸ Sort the words in the box according to common sounds.

ax	fax	quack	down	now	quill
lax	quints	flax	quilt	hour	wax

▸ Write similar-sounding words in each column on the template.

▸ After sorting, label the columns with the letters for the common sounds.

Exercise 1 · Listening for Sounds in Words

▸ Read each word.

▸ Fill in the chart with the number of letters and sounds in each word.

	How many letters are in the word?	How many sounds are in the word?
1. tax		
2. jazz		
3. quit		
4. ox		
5. six		
6. pill		
7. win		
8. boss		
9. ax		
10. sniff		

Exercise 2 · Spelling Pretest

▸ Write the words your teacher repeats.

1. _____   6. _____

2. _____   7. _____

3. _____   8. _____

4. _____   9. _____

5. _____   10. _____

Exercise 3 · Build It, Bank It

▸ Use the syllables **tox, ing, quilt, in, pact, land, sand, im, quick,** and **fill** to build two-syllable words.

▸ Write them on the lines below.

_____   _____

_____   _____

_____   _____

_____   _____

_____   _____

Exercise 4 · Classify It

▸ Use the vocabulary in the **Word Bank** below.

Word Bank

bobcat	rat	cod	crab	cat	yak
hog	squid	frog	rabbit	bass	dog

▸ Find words that go together based on their meaning.

▸ Fill in the blanks.

1. _____ and _____ are both _____ .

2. _____ and _____ are both _____ .

3. _____ and _____ are both _____ .

4. _____ and _____ are both _____ .

5. _____ and _____ are both _____ .

Exercise 5 · Code It: Subjects and Adjectives

▶ Listen as your teacher reads each sentence. Then:

- Write **S** over the noun that is the subject in each sentence.

- Underline the words that tell *how many, what kind,* or *which one.*

- Write **ADJ** above the underlined words or phrases.

Note: The first sentence is done for you.

         ADJ   S
1. The <u>dangerous</u> toxins spilled.

2. The mallard ducks by the pond quacked.

3. The lone fox stood still.

4. The box with the ribbon contained the gift.

5. Six wax candles burned in the window.

Exercise 6 · Diagram It 1 and 2: Subject/Predicate/Direct Object

▶ Fill in the diagrams with your teacher. Use the **Code It** (exercise 5) sentences.

1.

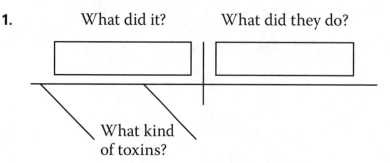

What did it?   What did they do?

What kind of toxins?

(continued)

Exercise 6 (continued) · Diagram It 1 and 2

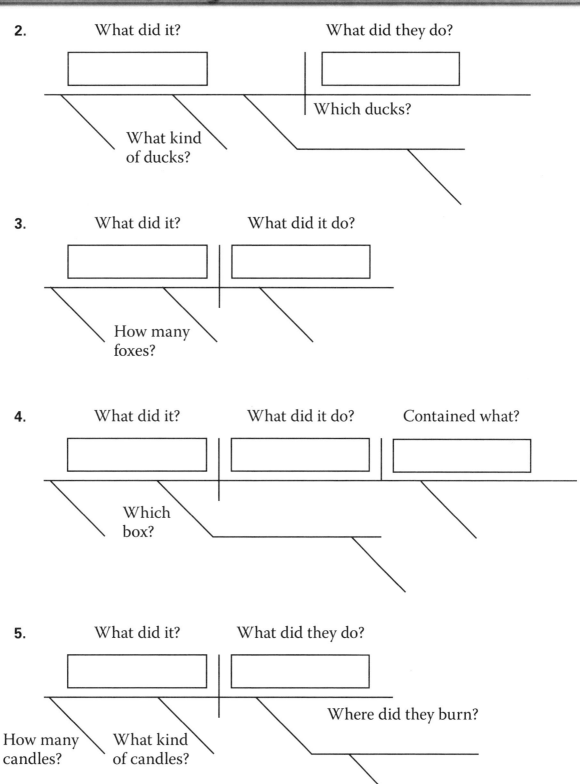

2.   What did it?   What did they do?

What kind of ducks?

Which ducks?

3.   What did it?   What did it do?

How many foxes?

4.   What did it?   What did it do?   Contained what?

Which box?

5.   What did it?   What did they do?

How many candles?   What kind of candles?

Where did they burn?

Unit 6 · Lesson 6

Exercise 7 · Answer It

▶ Underline the question word and answer these questions.

▶ Underline the part of the sentence that replaces the question word. For example, underline how something is done in answer to "how" questions.

1. How does toxic waste spoil everything?

_____

_____

_____

2. How do pesticides destroy our land?

_____

_____

_____

3. What happens when the air is polluted?

_____

_____

_____

4. How is acid rain created?

_____

_____

_____

5. How does acid rain harm the environment?

_____

_____

_____

Exercise 1 · Review: Doubling Rule

▶ Study the pattern of the words in the box.

quit	box	drill	fax	blot
crop	quack	log	quiz	mix

▶ Circle the words that follow the 1-1-1 pattern.

▶ Write the circled words in the first column of the **Double It** template.

▶ Spell the words with different suffixes.

▶ Mark as many columns on the **Double It** template as are appropriate.

Note: The letter **x** represents two sounds. It acts like two consonants in one.

Unit 6 · Lesson 7

Exercise 2 · Find It: Plural, Possessive, Present, or Progressive

▸ Listen as your teacher reads each row.

▸ Underline the targeted word or words.

Can you find...?	
Examples:	
Third person singular present tense verb	Toxic waste <u>infects</u> the land.
Present progressive verb	People <u>are dumping</u> poisons into the rivers.
Plural noun	Power <u>plants</u> can pollute the air.
Singular possessive noun	The <u>city's</u> landfill has a box to collect plastic.
1. Plural noun	Toxins can drift downwind of the plant.
2. Present progressive verb	Pesticide run-off is spilling into our lakes.
3. Singular possessive noun	Toxins sink into a frog's skin.
4. Third person singular present tense verb	A frog's skin tells scientists if the frog is well.
5. Third person singular present tense verb	A scientist tracks frogs to test their skin for pox and odd spots.
6. Singular possessive noun	The smog harms my dog's lungs.
7. Present progressive verb	My dog Fred is yapping like a sick duck.
8. Plural noun	The polluted air can make plants sick.
9. Third person singular present tense verbs	If polluted air drifts in, my dog gets ill.
10. Plural nouns	Rachel said to live in balance with plants and animals.

Exercise 3 · Rewrite It: Present to Present Progressive

▶ Review the present progressive verb form in the charts in the *Student Text*, pages 221–222.

▶ Listen as your teacher reads each present tense sentence in the first column below.

▶ Rewrite each sentence with a present progressive verb in the second column. Read the rewritten sentence to check your work.

Present Tense	Present Progressive Form
1. Acid rain falls from the sky.	
2. The acid rain drops on the land and in the water.	
3. The poisons kill fish in lakes.	
4. The poisons deform frogs in ponds.	
5. Gases from power plants and factories lift toxins into the air.	
6. The toxins collect in water.	
7. The toxins drip into the soil.	
8. Trees drop their leaves because of toxins in the acid rain.	
9. Crops get smaller because of toxins in the rain.	
10. Acid rain kills crops, fish, and trees.	

Unit 6 · Lesson 7

Exercise 4 · More Find It: Present Tense and Plurals

▸ Turn to **"Coming Clean About Toxic Pollution"** in the *Student Text*, page 201.

▸ Listen as your teacher reads the first section, **"Toxic Waste."**

▸ Find and list:

1. Present tense verbs (there are seven).

   _____   _____

   _____   _____

   _____   _____

   _____

2. Plural nouns (there are nine).

   _____   _____

   _____   _____

   _____   _____

   _____   _____

   _____

Exercise 5 · Sentence Dictation

▸ Listen as your teacher reads the sentences.

▸ Repeat each sentence and write it on the line.

▸ Circle the subject of the sentence.

▸ Underline words that describe the subject:

- adjectives or

- prepositional phrases that act as adjectives

1. _____

2. _____

3. _____

4. _____

5. _____

▸ Study the adjectives or prepositional phrases you underlined.

1. Write three words or phrases that tell *what kind*:

   _____

2. Write a word or phrase that tells *which one*: _____

▸ Write three examples of adjectives that tell *how many*:

_____

Exercise 6 · Blueprint for Reading

from "Coming Clean About Toxic Pollution"

Toxic Waste

Toxic waste spoils everything. It infects. It destroys. It destroys our land. It destroys our water. People dump poison. It gets into rivers. It gets into lakes. It even gets buried! Landfills are infected. Our land is damaged in other ways, too. Chemicals are sprayed. Pesticides get into the air. They get into the soil. It rains. The poison drains. It runs into rivers and lakes. It runs into oceans. Toxins are in the air. They are in the water. We are at risk. Our animals are at risk. Our land is at risk.

Air Pollution

What happens when the air is polluted? We breathe in poison. We can't always see the pollution. Sometimes, it hangs over a city. We can see a dirty mist. This mist is smog. Smog can cover a city. Fumes are harmful, too. They come from cars and trucks. They can make smog. Some cars have a special device. It changes poisons into less harmful gases. This cuts air pollution by 90 percent.

Acid Rain

How is acid rain created? It is created by exhaust. Gases come from factories. Gases come from power plants. Gases come from road vehicles. These gases react with sunlight. They react with air moisture. What is the result? They produce acid rain. When acid rain falls, it causes damage. It harms everything it touches. Poison levels in soil rise. Trees lose their leaves. Plants die. Statues are eaten away. In the lakes, fish die.

Exercise 7 · Blueprint for Writing

Exercise 1 · Syllable Awareness

▸ Listen to the word your teacher says.

▸ Count the syllables in the word.

▸ Write the letter for each vowel sound you hear.

	How many syllables do you hear?	First vowel sound	Second vowel sound	Third vowel sound
1.				
2.				
3.				
4.				
5.				
6.				
7.				
8.				
9.				
10.				

Exercise 2 · Listening for Word Parts

▸ Listen to each word.

▸ Write the word part your teacher repeats.

1. _____   3. _____   5. _____   7. _____   9. _____

2. _____   4. _____   6. _____   8. _____   10. _____

Exercise 3 · Word Networks: Antonyms, Synonyms, and Attributes

▸ Listen to each pair of words.

▸ How are these words related?

- Opposite meanings are **antonyms**.

- The same or similar meanings are **synonyms**.

- Features, such as size, shape, or action, are **attributes**.

▸ Put an X in the column to show the relationship.

Word pair	Antonym	Synonym	Attribute
1. fix: repair			
2. down: up			
3. duck: quack			
4. mix: blend			
5. box: lid			
6. now: later			
7. fox: tail			
8. toxic: poisonous			
9. wax: drip			
10. quitting: starting			

Unit 6 · Lesson 8

Exercise 4 · Diagram It 1 and 2: Subject/Predicate/Direct Object

▸ Use the sentences from Lesson 7, exercise 5 (Sentence Dictation).

▸ Write each sentence part in the diagram.

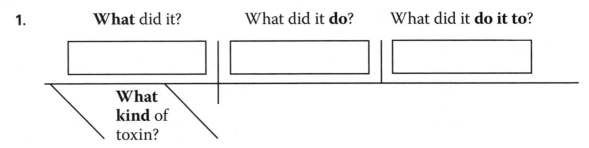

1. **What** did it?   What did it **do**?   What did it **do it to**?

    What kind of toxin?

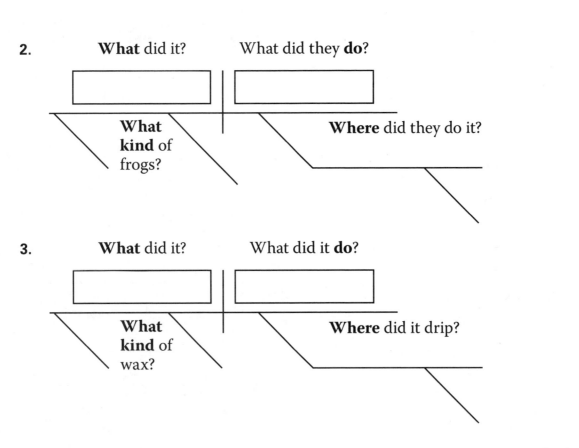

2. **What** did it?   What did they **do**?

    What kind of frogs?

    Where did they do it?

3. **What** did it?   What did it **do**?

    What kind of wax?

    Where did it drip?

(continued)

Exercise 4 (continued) · Diagram It 1 and 2

4.

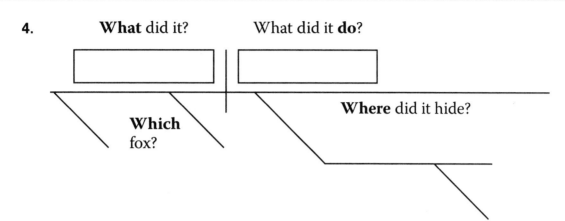

What did it?   What did it **do**?

Which fox?

Where did it hide?

5.

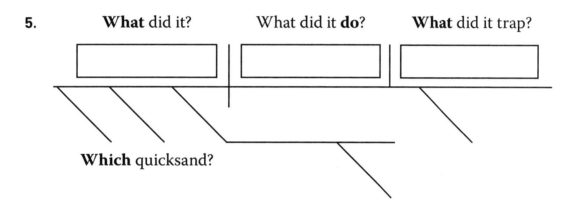

What did it?   What did it **do**?   **What** did it trap?

Which quicksand?

Exercise 5 · Blueprint for Reading

▸ Highlight walls and pictures in this text.

from "Coming Clean About Toxic Pollution"

River Pollution

How do rivers get polluted? There are toxins in our homes. What are the sources? Paint thinner. Cleaning supplies. Bug spray. Fertilizer. All of these contain toxins. Some toxins are washed down the drain. These toxins get into the sewers. They get into the soil. Then, the rain comes. The rain flushes out the toxins. Toxins wind up in rivers. There, they harm the fish.

Sea Pollution

Some plants dump chemicals. Where are they dumped? Some dump them into rivers. The poison flows downstream. It pours into the sea. Small fish feed on it. Small fish are eaten by bigger fish. Ocean mammals eat the bigger fish. What happens? The toxins poison the ocean. They destroy its life.

Dead Lakes

Toxins kill lakes. Farmers use fertilizers. They use huge amounts. Fertilizer is important. It increases their harvest. However, much is washed away. It gets into streams and lakes. This causes water plants, like algae, to grow in large numbers. This blocks out light. It uses up all the water's oxygen. Fish and other water animals need oxygen. There is not enough to support them. They die.

Exercise 6 · Blueprint for Writing

Exercise 1 · Listening for Sounds in Words

▶ Read each word.

▶ Fill in the chart with the number of letters and sounds in each word.

	How many letters are in the word?	How many sounds are in the word?
1. quick		
2. will		
3. picks		
4. sox		
5. quill		
6. fizz		
7. bog		
8. fax		
9. wick		
10. racks		

Exercise 2 · Sort It: Which One? What Kind? How Many?

▶ Listen to this selection as your teacher reads it.

▶ Decide if the underlined words and phrases tell:

- *which one,*

- *what kind,* or

- *how many*

▶ Write each underlined adjective or prepositional phrase in one of the template columns (next page) to show the question it answers.

---

from "Coming Clean About Toxic Pollution"

<u>Toxic</u> waste spoils everything. <u>Many</u> toxins destroy our land and water. People <u>from many places</u> dump poison. <u>These</u> toxins get into rivers and lakes. It even gets buried! Landfills are infected. Our land is damaged in other ways, too. Chemicals <u>with pesticides</u> are sprayed. From the spray, they get into the air. When it rains, the <u>dangerous</u> chemicals drop to the ground. It runs into streams, rivers, and lakes. Toxins are in the air. They are in the water. Toxins put people, plants, and animals at risk.

What happens when the air is polluted? We breathe in poison. We can't always see this <u>invisible</u> poison. Sometimes, it hangs over a city as a <u>dirty</u> mist. This mist is smog. Fumes <u>from cars and trucks</u> cause the smog. Smog can cover a city. Some cars have a special device. It changes poisons into less harmful gases. This cuts <u>air</u> pollution by 90 percent.

(continued)

Unit 6 · Lesson 9

Which one?	What kind?	How many?

Resources

Resources

Consonant Chart

Mouth Position

Type of Consonant Sound	Lips	Lips/Teeth	Tongue Between Teeth	Tongue Behind Teeth	Roof of Mouth	Back of Mouth	Throat
Stops							
Fricatives							
Affricatives							
Nasals							
Lateral							
Semivowels							

Letter-Sound Fluency

	Correct	Errors
1st Try		
2nd Try		

10	b	c	f	a	f	c	b	m	s	t
20	s	a	c	f	b	m	s	t	s	m
30	f	c	b	m	b	m	f	c	a	f
40	t	s	m	f	c	b	m	s	t	a
50	b	c	f	a	f	c	b	m	s	t
60	s	a	c	f	b	m	s	t	s	m
70	f	c	b	m	b	m	f	c	a	f
80	t	s	m	f	c	b	m	s	t	a
90	b	c	f	a	f	c	b	m	s	t
100	s	a	c	f	b	m	s	t	s	m

	Correct	Errors
1st Try		
2nd Try		

10	b	c	f	a	f	c	b	m	s	t
20	s	a	c	f	b	m	s	t	s	m
30	f	c	b	m	b	m	f	c	a	f
40	t	s	m	f	c	b	m	s	t	a
50	b	c	f	a	f	c	b	m	s	t
60	s	a	c	f	b	m	s	t	s	m
70	f	c	b	m	b	m	f	c	a	f
80	t	s	m	f	c	b	m	s	t	a
90	b	c	f	a	f	c	b	m	s	t
100	s	a	c	f	b	m	s	t	s	m

Unit 1 Fluency

Word Fluency 1

	Correct	Errors
1st Try		
2nd Try		

10	at	bat	sat	cat	cab	tab	cat	sat	bat	at
20	cat	at	cab	tab	at	cat	sat	bat	cab	tab
30	bat	tab	sat	cab	cat	cat	cab	tab	bat	sat
40	sat	tab	cab	bat	tab	cab	cat	bat	sat	at
50	cat	cab	cat	at	bat	tab	cab	sat	at	tab
60	bat	sat	at	tab	cat	cab	tab	cat	sat	bat
70	sat	bat	cat	cab	sat	tab	cab	at	bat	cab
80	bat	cab	sat	cat	at	bat	tab	cab	at	at
90	tab	sat	cat	bat	at	cat	at	tab	cat	sat
100	at	cat	bat	cab	sat	cat	at	bat	tab	cab

Word Fluency 2

		Correct	Errors
1st Try			
2nd Try			

cat	Sam	bam	mat	Sam	am	bam	cat	mat	fat	**10**
bam	fat	mat	cat	bam	fat	am	Sam	Sam	am	**20**
mat	am	cat	Sam	fat	bam	Sam	am	cat	cat	**30**
Sam	am	Sam	mat	am	Sam	bam	cat	mat	fat	**40**
Sam	am	fat	am	mat	Sam	cat	fat	cat	am	**50**
bam	Sam	am	bam	fat	am	bam	cat	bam	mat	**60**
mat	cat	Sam	cat	am	Sam	cat	fat	Sam	fat	**70**
cat	mat	bam	am	fat	mat	am	Sam	mat	Sam	**80**
mat	Sam	fat	am	Sam	fat	Sam	am	fat	cat	**90**
am	bam	mat	Sam	bam	cat	bam	mat	fat	Sam	**100**

Word Fluency 3

	Correct	Errors
1st Try		
2nd Try		

10	cat	mast	cast	mat	mast	mat	cast	cat	fast	fat
20	fast	fat	mat	cat	cast	fat	fast	mast	fat	fast
30	mat	fast	cat	mast	fat	cast	mast	fast	mat	cat
40	cat	cast	mast	mat	fast	mast	fast	mat	cat	fat
50	cast	mast	cast	fat	mat	fast	mast	cat	fat	fast
60	mat	cat	fat	fast	cast	mast	fast	cast	cat	mat
70	cat	mat	cast	mast	cat	fast	mast	fat	mat	mast
80	mat	mast	cat	cast	fast	fat	mat	mast	fast	fat
90	fast	cat	fast	mat	fat	mast	fast	fat	cast	cat
100	fat	cast	mat	mast	cat	cast	fat	mat	fast	mast

Word Fluency 4

	Correct	Errors
1st Try		
2nd Try		

#									
10	is	that	this	are	is	are	this	that	is
20	that	this	are	that	this	is	this	are	that
30	that	is	is	is	this	are	are	is	this
40	is	are	this	that	are	that	this	that	are
50	this	is	are	that	this	are	is	that	is
60	that	that	this	this	that	this	are	that	is
70	are	is	is	are	is	this	that	this	is
80	this	are	that	that	are	is	this	are	that
90	is	that	this	that	is	are	this	are	is
100	are	this	are	this	are	that	are	is	that

Phrase Fluency 1

Correct	Errors

1st Try / 2nd Try

a cat	2	sat on a cab	73
a fat cat	5	sat on a mat	77
a cab	7	that bat	79
a bat	9	that cat	81
at bat	11	that cab	83
fat cats	13	that mat	85
fat bats	15	that fat cat	88
bats at	17	the mat	90
bat at a ball	21	the cat	92
bats at the ball	25	the bat	94
has a cab	28	the cab	96
has a mat	31	the cats	98
has a cat	34	the mats	100
has a fat cat	38	the fat cats	103
has a cat	41	the fat bats	106
has cats	43	the bats	108
has bats	45	the cabs	110
a bat	47	this cat	112
a cab	49	this fat cat	115
in the cab	52	this bat	117
Casey in a cab	56	this fat bat	120
sat in a cab	60	this cab	122
on the cat	63	this mat	124
on the mat	66	the mat	126
in the cab	69	the bat	128

Phrase Fluency 2

Errors	
Correct	
1st Try	
2nd Try	

a cat	2	sat on a cab	79
a fat cat	5	sat on a mat	83
a fast cat	8	that bat	85
a fast cab	11	that cast	87
a fast bat	14	that fact	89
a fact	16	the acts	91
a bat	18	the cats	93
at bat	20	the cast	95
bat at a ball	24	the fast cabs	98
bat facts	26	the fact	100
bats at	28	the facts	102
bats at the ball	32	the fast bats	105
acts in the cast	36	the fat cats	108
in the act	39	the China cat	111
has a cab	42	the masts	113
has a cast	45	the mat	115
has a fast cat	49	the scab	117
has a scab	52	the scabs	119
in the act	55	the umpires	121
in the cab	58	this act	123
Casey in a cab	62	this cab	125
sat in a cab	66	this cast	127
on the cast	69	this mast	129
on the mast	72	this mat	131
in the cast	75	this scab	133

Unit 2 Fluency

Letter-Sound Fluency

	Correct	Errors
1st Try		
2nd Try		

10	t	m	a	s	p	j	r	h	l	n
20	j	r	n	l	n	b	f	a	t	s
30	a	r	h	n	l	h	r	j	s	p
40	h	j	a	b	f	c	t	m	s	a
50	s	m	a	s	p	j	r	h	l	n
60	n	l	h	r	j	s	p	f	c	t
70	t	m	a	s	p	j	r	h	l	n
80	j	r	n	l	n	b	f	c	t	s
90	b	a	h	n	l	h	r	j	s	p
100	t	m	a	s	p	j	r	h	l	n

Letter-Name Fluency

Correct	Errors
1st Try	
2nd Try	

t	m	a	s	p	j	h	l	n	**10**
j	r	n	l	n	b	f	a	t	s	**20**
a	r	h	n	l	h	r	j	s	p	**30**
h	j	a	b	f	c	t	m	s	a	n	**40**
s	m	a	s	p	j	h	l	n	**50**
n	l	h	r	j	s	p	f	c	l	t	**60**
t	m	a	s	p	j	h	l	n	**70**
j	r	n	l	n	b	c	j	r	s	s	**80**
b	a	h	n	l	h	r	j	s	p	**90**
t	m	a	s	p	j	h	l	n	**100**

Word Fluency 1

	Correct	Errors
1st Try		
2nd Try		

10	cap	nap	map	can	nap	tap	map	cap	can	an
20	map	an	can	cap	map	an	tap	nap	an	tap
30	can	tap	cap	nap	an	map	nap	tap	cap	cap
40	cap	map	nap	cap	tap	nap	map	cap	can	an
50	map	nap	map	an	can	tap	nap	cap	an	tap
60	can	cap	an	tap	map	nap	tap	map	cap	can
70	cap	can	map	nap	map	tap	nap	an	can	nap
80	can	nap	cap	map	tap	an	can	nap	tap	an
90	tap	cap	map	can	an	nap	tap	map	an	cap
100	an	can	map	nap	cap	map	an	can	tap	nap

	Correct	Errors
1st Try		
2nd Try		

am	jam	clam	has	jam	clam	ham	**10**
as	am	has	clam	ham	am	clam	**20**
ham	jam	as	am	has	ham	jam	**30**
am	ham	clam	as	ham	clam	ham	**40**
has	am	has	jam	am	has	clam	**50**
jam	clam	as	clam	as	ham	jam	**60**
has	am	has	clam	has	jam	ham	**70**
am	has	jam	as	clam	has	jam	**80**
ham	clam	as	am	jam	ham	as	**90**
has	jam	am	clam	has	clam	am	**100**

Word Fluency 3

	Correct	Errors
1st Try		
2nd Try		

10	plant	flap	fat	plan	flap	flat	fat	plant	plan	lap
20	fat	lap	plan	plant	fat	lap	flat	flap	lap	flat
30	plan	flat	plant	flap	lap	fat	flap	flat	plan	plant
40	plant	fat	flap	plan	flat	flap	fat	plan	plant	lap
50	fat	flap	fat	lap	plan	flat	flat	plant	lap	flat
60	plan	plant	lap	flat	fat	flat	fat	lap	plant	plan
70	plant	plan	fat	flap	plant	flat	flap	flap	plan	flap
80	plan	flap	plant	fat	flat	flat	flat	lap	flat	lap
90	flat	plant	fat	plan	flap	flat	fat	plan	fat	plant
100	lap	fat	plan	plant	plant	lap	plan	flat	plan	cat

Word Fluency 4

	Correct	Errors
1st Try		
2nd Try		

10	who	said	you	do	said	your	you	who	do	to
20	you	to	do	who	you	to	your	said	to	your
30	do	your	who	said	to	you	said	your	your	who
40	who	you	said	do	your	said	you	who	do	to
50	you	said	you	your	do	your	said	who	to	your
60	do	who	to	your	said	you	your	you	who	do
70	who	do	you	said	who	said	said	you	your	said
80	do	said	you	your	your	to	do	to	your	to
90	your	who	you	do	said	your	your	you	to	who
100	to	you	do	said	who	you	to	who	do	cat

Phrase Fluency 1

	Correct	Errors
1st Try		
2nd Try		

the lab	2	has a lab	66
at the lab	5	has a rat	69
has a lab	8	has a man	72
a lab	10	has a cap	75
your lab	12	has sap	77
your lap	14	in the cab	80
your pal	16	in the lab	83
your pan	18	in your lab	86
into the pan	21	do your	88
into the lab	24	pat your	90
into the cab	27	Pat has	92
into the river	30	has the hat	95
in a jam	33	has the map	98
your jam	35	has the jam	101
can jam	37	has your cap	104
that jam	39	has your ham	107
can nap	41	has your hat	110
a nap	43	has that	112
cat naps	45	has this	114
said the man	48	has to	116
said the tan man	52	has to do	119
to the man	55	can do	121
to can	57	can cap	123
to the fan	60	can tap	125
to the lab	63	can map	127

Phrase Fluency 2

the lamp	2	has a plan	69
on the lamp	5	has a plant	72
has a lamp	8	has a past	75
a lamp	10	has a mast	78
your lamp	12	who has	80
your plan	14	who is	82
your plant	16	who do	84
your scalp	18	do you	86
into the plant	21	do your	88
into the craft	24	said your	90
into the past	27	your snaps	92
into the river	30	has snaps	94
in a river	33	has the plan	97
on a raft	36	has the plant	100
can raft	38	has your clam	103
rafts can	40	has your clamp	106
on the ramp	43	has a blast	109
your ramp	45	has that	111
the man's ramp	48	has this	113
said the plant man	52	has to do	116
said the tan man	56	has crafts	118
said the scrap man	60	can do crafts	121
last man	62	can scrap	123
last fan	64	can scan	125
last lab	66	can scan maps	128

Unit 3 Fluency

Letter-Sound Fluency

Correct	Errors
1st Try	
2nd Try	

10	i	a	v	d	g	a	i	v	g	d
20	a	r	h	n	l	h	r	j	s	p
30	h	j	a	b	f	v	d	g	a	i
40	s	m	a	s	p	j	r	h	l	n
50	n	l	h	a	i	v	d	c	t
60	v	d	g	a	i	j	r	h	l	n
70	j	r	n	l	a	i	v	g	d	s
80	b	a	h	n	l	h	j	s	p
90	t	m	a	s	p	r	h	l	n
100	a	i	v	g	d	v	d	g	a	i

284 Unit 3 • Fluency

	Correct	Errors
1st Try		
2nd Try		

10	i	a	v	g	d	a	i	v	g	d
20	a	r	h	n	l	h	r	j	s	p
30	h	j	a	b	f	g	d	v	a	i
40	s	m	a	s	p	j	r	h	l	n
50	n	l	h	a	d	v	g	i	c	t
60	v	d	g	a	i	j	h	r	d	n
70	j	r	n	l	a	i	v	v	j	s
80	b	a	h	n	h	h	r	j	s	p
90	t	m	a	s	j	r	r	h	l	n
100	a	i	v	g	v	d	d	g	a	i

Word Fluency 1

	Correct	Errors
1st Try		
2nd Try		

10	dig	big	did	dim	big	hid	did	dig	dim	him
20	did	him	dim	dig	did	him	hid	big	him	hid
30	dim	hid	dig	big	him	did	big	hid	dim	dig
40	dig	did	big	dim	hid	big	dig	dim	dig	him
50	did	big	did	him	dim	hid	big	hid	him	hid
60	dim	dig	him	hid	big	big	dig	did	did	dig
70	dig	dim	did	big	dig	hid	big	him	big	dim
80	dim	big	dig	did	hid	gad	gab	big	hid	him
90	hid	dig	did	him	big	big	him	hid	did	dig
100	big	hid	dim	big	dig	did	him	dim	did	hid

Word Fluency 2

	Correct	Errors
1st Try		
2nd Try		

fit	lift	fig	bit	gift	fig	fit	bit	big	10
fig	big	bit	fit	big	big	gift	lift	gift	20
bit	gift	fit	lift	fig	lift	gift	bit	fit	30
fit	gift	lift	fit	gift	fig	bit	fig	big	40
fig	lift	fig	big	bit	gift	lift	big	gift	50
bit	fit	big	fig	lift	lift	gift	fit	bit	60
fit	bit	fig	lift	fit	gift	lift	big	lift	70
bit	lift	fit	gift	big	gift	bit	lift	big	80
gift	fit	fig	big	lift	big	gift	gift	fit	90
big	fig	bit	lift	fit	fig	big	bit	lift	100

Word Fluency 3

	Correct	Errors
1st Try		
2nd Try		

10	hand	flag	brag	have	flag	brag	brand	hand	have	had
20	brand	had	have	brand	brag	had	brand	flag	had	brag
30	have	brag	hand	flag	had	brand	flag	brag	have	hand
40	hand	brand	flag	have	brag	flag	brand	have	hand	had
50	brand	flag	brand	had	have	brag	flag	hand	had	brag
60	have	hand	had	brag	brand	flag	brag	brand	hand	have
70	hand	have	brand	flag	hand	brag	flag	flag	have	flag
80	have	flag	have	hand	brand	had	brand	have	brag	had
90	brag	brand	brand	have	had	flag	brag	had	brand	hand
100	had	brand	have	flag	hand	brand	had	have	brag	flag

Word Fluency 4

was	were	of	from	they	what	were	of	10
they	was	what	they	was	from	of	from	20
of	were	they	what	from	was	what	were	30
was	of	were	from	what	they	were	of	40
they	was	of	what	they	were	was	from	50
were	of	from	they	what	from	they	were	60
what	were	was	of	they	of	what	of	70
was	they	what	gab	gad	they	were	were	80
of	from	was	they	what	was	from	they	90
what	they	were	was	from	of	were	what	100

Fluency

Phrase Fluency 1

	Correct	Errors
1st Try		
2nd Try		

the dig	2	has a big van	63
the big dig	5	who has a	66
dig it	7	who bit	68
can dig	9	who did	70
dig that	11	who had	72
to dig	13	who hit	74
dig from	15	do hit	76
hid from	17	if they	78
grab from	19	if you	80
from him	21	if you do	83
from his	23	if your	85
from you	25	if this	87
was from	27	if that is	90
was I	29	if it is	93
was fit	31	is that	95
was bit	33	is your	97
was mad	35	is that your	100
was from dad	38	is that from	103
dad's bag	40	is this	105
dad's big bag	43	it lit	107
dad's dig bag	46	lit it	109
in the bag	49	mad at it	112
in the pit	52	nag at it	115
were in a pit	56	rig it	117
in this pit	59	dig it	119

Correct	Errors
1st Try	2nd Try

the last trip	3	the mint plant	65
the big trip	6	has a mint	68
of the trip	9	has a plant	71
trip from	11	has to plant	74
your trip	13	has to print	77
your plan	15	print a bit	80
your plant	17	plant a bit	83
your band	19	give a bit	86
your bad band	22	have a bit	89
the drab band	25	give a misfit	92
give the band	28	had a mishap	95
give him	30	was a mishap	98
give in	32	hid the mishap	101
give this	34	hid the van	104
give your dad	37	hid in the attic	108
give who	39	in the attic	111
gift from	41	a damp attic	114
drift from	43	attic fan	116
drift from it	46	big attic fan	119
hit the drift	49	candid fan	121
hit the grid	52	candid bandit	123
hit the strip	55	bad bandit	125
lift the strip	58	give the bandit	128
land from	60	flip the bandit	131
land this	62	flip it	133

Letter-Sound Fluency

Correct	Errors											
1st Try	2nd Try											

12	y	w	-ck	i	a	z	y	w	-ck	k
22	a	r	h	n	l	h	r	j	s	p
32	h	j	a	b	v	d	g	a	i	i
43	s	m	i	z	y	w	-ck	w	k	n
53	n	l	a	a	g	v	d	g	c	t
63	v	d	g	a	i	j	r	h	l	n
74	a	z	y	w	i	k	v	g	d	s
84	b	a	h	n	l	h	r	j	s	p
95	t	m	a	s	a	z	y	w	-ck	k
105	a	i	v	g	d	v	d	g	a	i

Letter-Name Fluency

	Correct	Errors
1st Try		
2nd Try		

10	y	w	c	i	a	y	z	w	c	k
20	a	r	h	n	l	h	r	j	s	p
30	h	j	a	b	f	v	d	w	z	y
40	s	m	i	a	y	w	z	k	c	n
50	n	l	h	z	w	v	g	d	w	t
60	v	d	k	a	i	y	w	z	n	n
70	a	z	y	w	c	k	v	g	s	s
80	b	a	h	n	l	h	r	j	p	p
90	t	m	a	s	a	z	y	w	c	k
100	a	y	v	g	k	v	d	g	w	z

Fluency

Word Fluency 1

	Correct	Errors
1st Try		
2nd Try		

10	stick	back	stack	black	stick	slick	slack	lack	pack	back
20	black	slack	lack	stack	slick	lack	black	stack	slack	pack
30	stick	lack	slick	back	stack	stick	slick	back	pack	stick
40	black	stack	back	slick	lack	stack	pack	black	slack	pack
50	lack	back	slack	stack	slick	lack	stick	pack	black	back
60	back	stack	stick	black	stick	slack	slick	black	stack	pack
70	black	lack	stack	slack	slick	stick	slack	pack	slick	lack
80	lack	black	pack	slick	back	stack	stick	slack	pack	back
90	black	stick	back	lack	stack	slack	black	pack	slick	stick
100	back	black	slack	slick	slack	lack	pack	stack	back	slick

	Correct	Errors
1st Try		
2nd Try		

pack	pick	kick	kid	skid	skin	tack	task	pack	skin	10
pick	pick	task	tack	kick	skid	task	kick	kid	tack	20
skin	skin	pack	skid	skin	task	pack	skid	kick	shin	30
pick	pick	tack	pick	task	kick	skid	pack	task	tack	40
pack	pack	pick	skin	skid	skid	task	kid	pack	kick	50
pick	pick	task	skid	kid	skin	tack	skin	task	pack	60
kick	kick	pick	kid	skin	skid	kid	task	kick	tack	70
pack	pack	pick	skin	task	pack	skid	pick	tack	kick	80
skin	skin	pick	tack	kid	task	kick	pack	skin	tack	90
skid	skid	task	pick	kick	kid	skid	kid	tack	pack	100

Word Fluency 3

	Correct	Errors
1st Try		
2nd Try		

10	swim	wag	twig	twin	swim	swift	twist	wind	wig	wag
20	twin	twist	wind	twig	swift	wind	twin	twig	twist	wig
30	swim	wind	swift	wag	twig	swim	swift	wag	wig	swim
40	twin	twig	wag	swift	wind	twig	wind	twin	twig	wig
50	wind	wag	twist	twig	swift	wind	swim	twin	wig	wag
60	wag	twig	swim	swim	twist	swift	twist	twin	twig	wig
70	twin	wind	twig	twist	swim	swift	swim	twist	swift	wind
80	wind	twin	swift	wag	twig	wag	swim	wig	wig	wag
90	twin	swim	wag	twig	twist	wind	twig	twin	wig	swim
100	wag	twin	twist	swift	swift	wind	twist	wig	twig	swift

	Correct	Errors
1st Try		
2nd Try		

be	he	does	she	when	does	she	we	he	be	10
when	we	when	be	when	he	we	does	we	when	20
does	she	he	he	we	be	he	we	she	does	30
we	he	be	when	he	does	be	when	he	we	40
we	she	he	we	be	does	when	he	we	we	50
she	when	does	he	we	be	he	she	when	we	60
he	she	when	he	we	we	she	be	when	he	70
when	she	we	she	does	be	he	she	we	when	80
does	he	he	does	she	be	be	does	he	does	90
we	be	does	he	be	does	be	when	he	she	100

Phrase Fluency 1

	Correct	Errors
1st Try		
2nd Try		

the twins	2	pet film	71
was a twin	5	pet pig	73
his twin	7	pet cats	75
was his twin	10	pig and cats	78
had a twin	13	your pig	80
had hits	15	your cats	82
had big hits	18	your pack	84
big hits	20	pack of pets	87
big twins	22	the pets	89
had fans	24	the pack	91
fans of twins	27	the pals	93
twin fans	29	are pals	95
were the twins	32	fit pals	97
when the twins	35	fit twins	99
twins were	37	swift twins	101
twins who	39	swift and fit pals	105
give the twins	42	fit fans	107
have the twins	45	big fan	109
your twins	47	big facts	111
you twins	49	plant facts	113
are twins	51	are facts	115
his twin	53	are plants	117
his lid	55	are plants facts	120
flip the lid	58	are fans	122
fans flip	60	are big fans	125
the fans	62	are fit twins	128
the film	64	trim twins	130
hit films	66	trim fans	132
in hit films	69	trim pals	134

Phrase Fluency 2

	Correct	Errors
1st Try		
2nd Try		

in the sky	3	plan trips	76
in the vast sky	7	to plan trips	79
in the past	10	in the plans	82
from the past	13	in the past	85
your past	15	in fact	87
in the past	18	lack of facts	90
was past	20	the fact	92
is past	22	his facts	94
is a twin	25	the fact is	97
twin plants	27	does the fact	100
twin kids	29	does the trick	103
your twin kids	32	a sick trick	106
for the Twins	35	was a trick	109
plan for Twins	38	was the sky	112
plan a trip	41	scan the sky	115
to plan trips	44	the scan	117
to plan	46	the task	119
to plant	48	his task	121
to plant sprigs	51	when his task	124
the twin plants	54	when the task	127
the plants	56	does the task	130
the plant	58	does the sky	133
the twin plant	61	does the plan	136
the twin	63	does the past	139
the plan	65	in the past	142
the fans	67	are fit twins	145
the film	69	trim twins	147
hit films	71	trim fans	149
in hit films	74	trim pals	151

Sentence Fluency 1

Errors		Elvis and his twin were born in 1935.	8
		His twin was Elvis. Elvis had 18 #1 hits.	17
Correct		Fans "flip their lids" for him.	23
		Elvis was in hit films.	28
		His pad was in Graceland.	33
1st Try	2nd Try	What did Elvis win?	37

Elvis and his twin are at Graceland.	44
Elvis is famous. Ask a fan if he lives!	53
She is Kim's twin.	57
Where do the twins live?	62
They have a pack of pets.	68
The twins have cats, horses, and a pig!	76
The twins are connected. Kim has tasks.	83
The twins are fit.	87
The twins admit they are pals.	93
The twins trim the horses.	98
The twins split plants.	102
It is crisp and brisk.	107
Kim said they can.	111
Kim's twin is a big fan of Kim's.	119
Kim is a big fan of her twin!	127
It is "Facts About Twins."	132

Sentence Fluency 2

The twin is in the vast sky.	7
It has twins.	10
It is abstract.	13
What did he name it?	18
Its name was the twin plants.	24
It stands for the Twins.	29
It stands for a ram.	34
It stands for a crab.	39
It was in the past.	44
They used them to plan trips.	50
They map the stars.	54
When did they plant?	58
A man can plant sprigs.	63
They were used to plan trips and to plant sprigs.	73
It splits the sky into segments.	79
His task is to scan the sky.	86
His task is to name the stars.	93
It tilts and spins.	97
In the vast sky, it is dim.	104
It is used to transmit facts.	110
It has twin stars.	114
We hit the twins, the ram and the crab.	123
It tilts and spins.	127
It transmits facts.	130

Letter-Sound Fluency

	Correct	Errors
1st Try		
2nd Try		

										Count
o	-ll	-ss	-ff	-zz	-ng	a	i	o	-ng	16
p	s	j	r	h	l	n	h	r	a	26
-ll	-ss	-ff	-zz	-ng	a	i	o	j	h	41
n	k	-ck	w	y	z	a	i	m	s	52
t	c	-ll	-ss	-ff	-zz	-ng	a	i	o	67
n	l	h	r	j	i	a	g	d	v	77
o	-ll	-ss	-ff	-zz	-ng	a	i	z	a	92
p	s	j	r	h	l	n	h	a	b	102
k	-ck	w	y	z	a	s	a	m	t	113
i	a	o	-ll	-ss	-ff	-zz	-ng	a	i	128

Letter-Name Fluency

	Correct	Errors
1st Try		
2nd Try		

10	g	i	a	n	z	f	s	l	o
20	a	r	h	l	h	r	j	o	p
30	h	j	o	i	o	l	n	z	f
40	s	m	i	a	y	w	k	o	n
50	o	i	a	g	z	l	s	c	t
60	v	d	g	a	i	r	h	l	n
70	a	z	i	o	g	n	s	g	o
80	b	a	h	n	l	r	j	s	p
90	t	m	o	s	z	y	w	c	k
100	i	a	l	n	z	g	o	a	i

Fluency

Word Fluency 1

	Correct	Errors
1st Try		
2nd Try		

10	fog	dog	frog	fog	dog	dock	dot	pod	nod	not
20	dog	dock	nod	frog	dock	not	dog	nod	dot	pod
30	fog	dot	pod	nod	dog	frog	not	fog	frog	dock
40	dog	fog	dot	dock	frog	pod	nod	not	dock	frog
50	frog	nod	nod	fog	dock	frog	not	pod	dot	nod
60	fog	dot	frog	frog	fog	nod	dot	dock	pod	not
70	dock	dog	nod	dock	dot	frog	not	dog	dog	dock
80	fog	pod	frog	dog	nod	frog	fog	dog	fog	pod
90	dock	frog	not	fog	dog	dot	fog	pod	dock	nod
100	frog	dog	nod	fog	pod	not	dog	nod	frog	fog

	Correct	Errors
1st Try		
2nd Try		

#										
10	sock	spot	spill	sill	loss	cost	lost	frost	cost	lost
20	spill	sill	spot	cost	sock	loss	frost	spot	loss	cost
30	loss	frost	lost	sock	frost	cost	spot	spill	sill	lost
40	frost	loss	sock	sock	spill	frost	loss	sill	lost	cost
50	spot	sill	spill	sock	frost	loss	lost	spot	cost	frost
60	sock	spill	loss	sill	spot	lost	frost	spill	sill	lost
70	loss	spot	cost	sock	frost	sill	loss	spot	cost	loss
80	spill	lost	lost	frost	sock	spot	cost	frost	spill	lost
90	spot	loss	spill	lost	sill	cost	lost	sock	frost	loss
100	lost	frost	spot	cost	sock	spill	lost	spot	cost	frost

Word Fluency 3

	Correct	Errors
1st Try		
2nd Try		

	10	20	30	40	50	60	70	80	90	100
	grill	gloss	loss	mass	glass	loss	gloss	mass	class	glass
	class	class	glass	loss	grass	glass	loss	grill	grass	mass
	grill	glass	mass	moss	class	gloss	grill	glass	moss	class
	grass	grass	class	glass	class	grass	loss	moss	grill	grass
	mass	moss	gloss	grill	gloss	moss	class	gloss	grass	loss
	moss	loss	grass	gloss	moss	grill	grass	loss	loss	moss
	loss	grass	moss	class	mass	gloss	moss	class	gloss	glass
	gloss	glass	loss	grass	grass	loss	class	grass	mass	grill
	glass	mass	grill	moss	loss	mass	grill	mass	class	gloss
	class	gloss	mass	grill	glass	class	mass	moss	glass	mass

Word Fluency 4

	Correct	Errors
1st Try		
2nd Try		

there	these	those	here	where	why	these	here	why	there	10
those	where	there	those	why	these	here	where	why	here	20
where	there	those	here	these	why	those	there	where	these	30
why	where	there	here	those	where	these	why	those	here	40
those	why	here	where	there	these	why	those	where	there	50
here	those	where	why	these	there	those	here	there	where	60
these	where	why	those	there	here	where	why	those	there	70
where	these	these	there	why	those	there	where	why	here	80
these	where	there	why	here	those	those	here	those	why	90
where	these	why	here	there	those	here	where	why	there	100

Phrase Fluency 1

		Correct	Errors
1st Try			
2nd Try			

what is	2	jazz lists	59
what are	4	on the list	62
what were	6	those lists	64
what was	8	these lists	66
where is	10	past lists	68
where was	12	the past	70
where are	14	past strands	72
where were	16	gives the strands	75
there were	18	give the list	78
there is	20	give the facts	81
there are	22	give a gift	84
there was	24	give these gifts	87
was jazz	26	give this gift	90
pick jazz	28	gift of music	93
jazz bands	30	fit and trim	96
these jazz bands	33	has music	98
those jazz bands	36	has skits	100
classic jazz bands	39	has slapstick	102
fantastic bands	41	has the band	105
fantastic jazz bands	44	for the band	108
fantastic impact	46	for the cast	111
impact on rock	49	for the hat	114
impact on rap	52	top hats	116
impact on hip-hop	55	top hat	118
impacts jazz	57	black top hat	121

Phrase Fluency 2

jazz is	2	lost past	58
jazz was	4	lost the past	61
here is	6	is not lost	64
here was	8	is not past	67
why is	10	past lists	69
why was	12	the past	71
why are	14	past strands	73
where were	16	impact the strands	76
there were	18	twist the strands	79
were brisk	20	twisting the strands	82
were fast	22	jazz twists	84
fast and brisk	25	a new twist	87
were fast and brisk	29	a new jazz twist	91
spin fast	31	jazz is	93
fast fans	33	jazz has	95
fast kicks	35	has the band	98
fast spins	37	has the fans	101
fast kicks and spins	41	has the music	104
backdrop kick	43	jazz music	106
sad backdrop	45	jazz band	108
drop-kicking	46	abstract jazz	110
kicking back	48	had to jazz	113
kick back and jam	52	had to sit	116
kicking past	54	sitting still	118
the past	56	still a hit	121

Sentence Fluency 1

	Correct	Errors	
1st Try			
2nd Try			

What is jazz? Jazz is music.	6
Rock is a kind of music.	12
Rap is music.	15
It is played. It is sung.	21
It is on a stand.	26
They stick to the written music.	32
Jazz bands do not.	36
Critics said it was strict.	41
The critics pick jazz.	45
It is classic!	48
It has had an impact.	53
The impact is fantastic!	57
The classics had an impact on rock.	64
They had an impact on rap.	70
They had an impact on hip-hop!	76
What is on the list?	81
The past gives the strands.	86
Music from the past impacts jazz.	92
Digging was a hot, drab task.	98
Picking crops was a hot job.	104
They did the tasks to music.	110
They were glad to have it.	116
They got the crops in fast.	122
It is a story. The facts are not valid.	131
It is a gift. It is music.	138
It has music. It has skits.	144
It has slapstick. The fans stomp.	150
They clap for the band.	155

Sentence Fluency 2

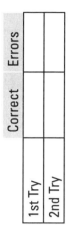

	It is fast. It is brisk.	6
	Fans spin.	8
	They kick to the music.	13
	The backdrop is a sad past.	19
	Bands ad-lib.	21
	They kick back and jam.	26
	In jazz, the past is not lost.	33
	The strands live on.	37
	What impact did they have?	42
	Jazz adds a new twist.	47
	Jazz is a hit.	51
	Fans flock to it.	55
	It has the band.	59
	It has the fans.	63
	It is vivid.	66
	The art is abstract.	70
	It gives jazz a "fabric."	75
	Its fabric is abstract.	79
	The band had to sit still.	85
	The film was not fast.	90
	It was not candid.	94
	It is jazz.	97
	Its fabric is vivid.	101
	Jazz is the topic.	105
	The past lives in jazz.	110
	The fabric of jazz is vivid.	116
	Jazz is still a hit.	121
	It is not a fad.	126
	In fact, it's a new classic!	132

Letter-Sound Fluency

	Correct	Errors
1st Try		
2nd Try		

10	-ng	o	i	a	-ng	-zz	-ff	-ss	-ll	o
20	a	r	h	x	l	h	r	j	qu	p
30	h	j	o	i	a	-ng	-zz	-ff	-ss	-ll
40	x	qu	i	a	z	y	w	-ck	k	n
50	o	i	a	-ng	-zz	-ff	-ss	-ll	c	qu
60	v	d	g	a	i	j	a	h	l	x
70	a	z	i	a	-ng	-zz	-ff	-ss	-ll	o
80	b	a	h	qu	l	h	r	j	x	p
90	t	m	qu	x	a	z	y	-ck	w	k
100	i	a	-ng	-zz	-ff	-ss	-ll	o	x	qu

Letter-Name Fluency

	Correct	Errors
1st Try		
2nd Try		

x	b	f	t	qu	m	s	x	o		11
a	h	x	l	h	r	j	qu	p		22
h	o	p	j	r	h	l	n	x		32
x	i	a	j	w	w	k	k	n		43
o	a	z	z	y	g	c	c	qu		54
v	d	a	v	d	j	h	l	x		64
a	z	a	i	f	t	qu	m	o		75
b	a	qu	b	h	r	j	x	p		86
t	m	x	qu	z	y	w	k	k		97
i	a	p	j	h	l	x	o	qu		108

Word Fluency 1

	Correct	Errors
1st Try		
2nd Try		

fax	fix	wax	flax	fax	sax	ax	six	mix	fix	10
flax	ax	six	wax	sax	six	flax	wax	ax	mix	20
fax	six	sax	fix	wax	fax	sax	mix	fix	fax	30
flax	wax	fix	sax	six	wax	fix	flax	ax	mix	40
six	fix	ax	wax	sax	six	mix	fax	flax	fix	50
fix	wax	fax	flax	fax	ax	sax	flax	wax	mix	60
flax	six	wax	ax	sax	fax	wax	ax	mix	six	70
six	flax	mix	sax	fix	fax	wax	fax	ax	fix	80
flax	fax	fix	six	six	ax	flax	fix	mix	fax	90
fix	flax	ax	sax	ax	mix	flax	ax	wax	sax	100

Word Fluency 2

	Correct	Errors
1st Try		
2nd Try		

#	Words									
10	quick	quit	quiz	quip	fox	box	toxic	toxin	quick	box
20	quit	quip	toxin	toxic	quiz	fox	toxic	quiz	toxin	quip
30	box	quit	quick	fox	box	toxin	quick	fox	quiz	toxic
40	quit	quip	toxic	quit	quip	quiz	fox	quick	toxin	box
50	quick	toxic	quit	box	quiz	fox	toxin	quip	quick	quiz
60	quit	toxin	toxic	fox	box	quip	toxic	box	toxin	quick
70	quiz	fox	toxin	quip	box	fox	toxin	toxin	quiz	toxic
80	quick	quit	quip	quip	box	quick	fox	quit	toxic	quiz
90	box	quit	quit	toxic	quip	quiz	toxin	quick	box	toxic
100	fox	quick	toxin	quit	quiz	quip	fox	quip	toxic	quick

Word Fluency 3

	Correct	Errors
1st Try		
2nd Try		

quill	tax	quint	quilt	quill	quick	quack	axis	lax	tax	**10**
quack	quint	axis	quilt	quick	axis	quilt	quint	quack	lax	**20**
quilt	axis	quick	tax	quint	quill	quick	tax	lax	quill	**30**
quill	quint	tax	quick	axis	quack	lax	quilt	quack	lax	**40**
axis	tax	quack	quint	quilt	axis	quill	quint	quilt	tax	**50**
tax	quint	quill	quilt	quick	quack	lax	quilt	quint	lax	**60**
quilt	axis	quint	quick	quill	quick	tax	quack	quick	axis	**70**
axis	quilt	lax	quick	tax	quilt	lax	quack	lax	tax	**80**
quilt	quill	tax	axis	quack	quilt	lax	quick	lax	quill	**90**
tax	quilt	quack	quack	quick	axis	lax	quack	quint	quick	**100**

	Correct	Errors
1st Try		
2nd Try		

10	how	for	her	now	for	me	her	down	now	how
20	her	for	me	her	now	for	down	how	me	down
30	now	me	how	down	for	now	down	me	how	me
40	her	down	for	now	me	down	her	how	for	for
50	how	me	down	now	how	how	me	her	for	down
60	me	how	her	down	how	now	for	me	down	her
70	how	down	for	me	down	how	down	for	me	now
80	her	for	me	down	how	for	her	how	her	me
90	for	down	her	down	how	her	how	for	how	now
100	how	for	me	how	down	me	her	her	how	me

Phrase Fluency

Errors	
Correct	
1st Try	2nd Try

her plot	2	plants for me	70
her land	4	facts for me	73
plot of land	7	printing facts	75
her plot of land	11	facts about combat	78
her plots	13	facts about rabbits	81
her crops	15	facts about rats	84
had crops	17	facts about rocks	87
had to ask for crops	22	the rock	89
had to ask	25	six rocks	91
had rabbits	27	six robins	93
her rabbits	29	kill robins	95
her rats	31	toxic robins	97
quick rats	33	toxic land	99
quick rabbits	35	toxic crops	101
her quick rabbits	38	give crops	103
her quick rats	41	had to give	106
six quick rabbits	44	had to print	109
her rats and rabbits	48	had to stop	112
facts about rabbits	51	had to tax	115
facts about plants	54	to limit	117
plant mix	56	have to ban	120
six plants	58	have to limit	123
in the plants	61	her limit	125
in the pond	64	for the limit	128
in the plants	67	for the land	131

Sentence Fluency

	Correct	Errors
1st Try		
2nd Try		

I am Miss Rachel Carson.	5
The plot of land was vast.	12
I had to ask mom.	17
I got the facts about rabbits and rats.	25
We got to track them in the plants.	33
In the pond, we could spot bass and frogs.	42
I will win a grant.	47
I admit I did.	51
I split the rock.	55
It had the imprint on it.	61
In the lab, we studied the plan in a frog.	71
What can kill robins?	75
I had plans to fix the impact of DDT.	84
I was a bit timid.	89
The facts prompt me to act.	95
I had to give the facts.	101
I had to print them.	106
The facts must stop the quick profit.	113
The land is vast.	117
The cost to the land is vast.	124
The task is to stop toxins.	130
They said toxins can kill.	135
Toxic pollution is bad.	139
We have to ban DDT and limit toxins.	147

Fluency Charts

Correct Letter-Sounds per Minute

Unit:

Dates:

10 20 30 40 50 60 70 80 90 100 110

Letter-Name Fluency Chart

Correct Letter-Names per Minute

110
100
90
80
70
60
50
40
30
20
10

Dates:

Unit:

Fluency Charts

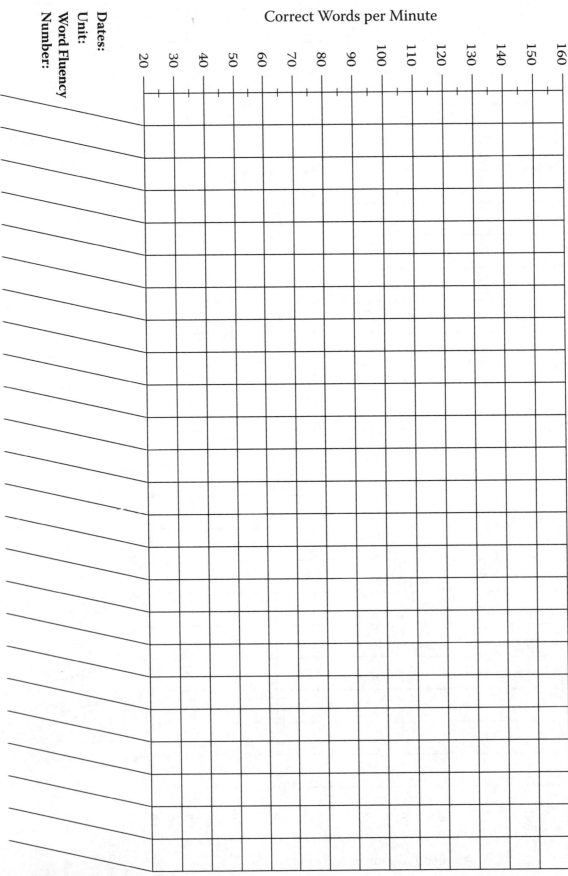

Correct Words per Minute

Dates:
Unit:
Word Fluency
Number:

Word Fluency Chart

Correct Words per Minute

160
150
140
130
120
110
100
90
80
70
60
50
40
30
20

Dates:
Unit:
Word Fluency
Number:

Fluency Charts

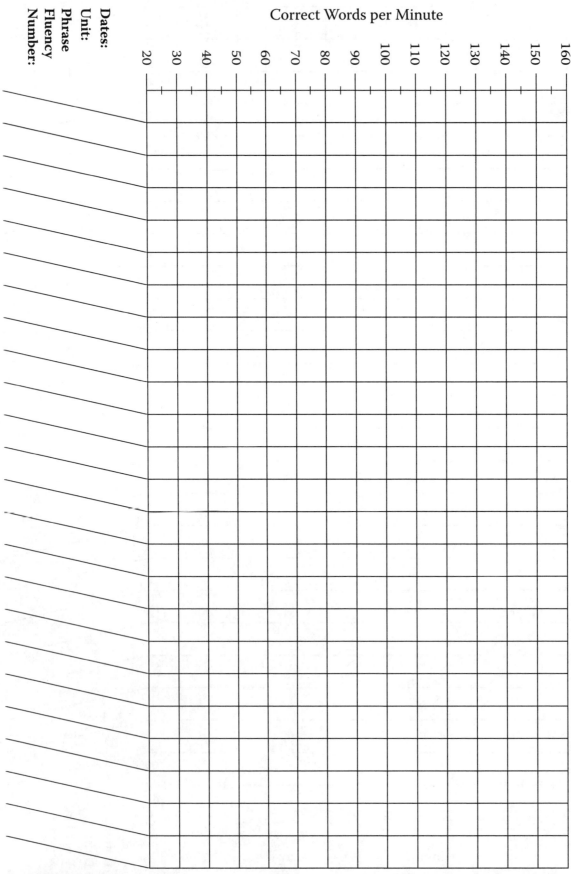

Correct Words per Minute

20 30 40 50 60 70 80 90 100 110 120 130 140 150 160

Dates:
Unit:
Phrase
Fluency
Number:

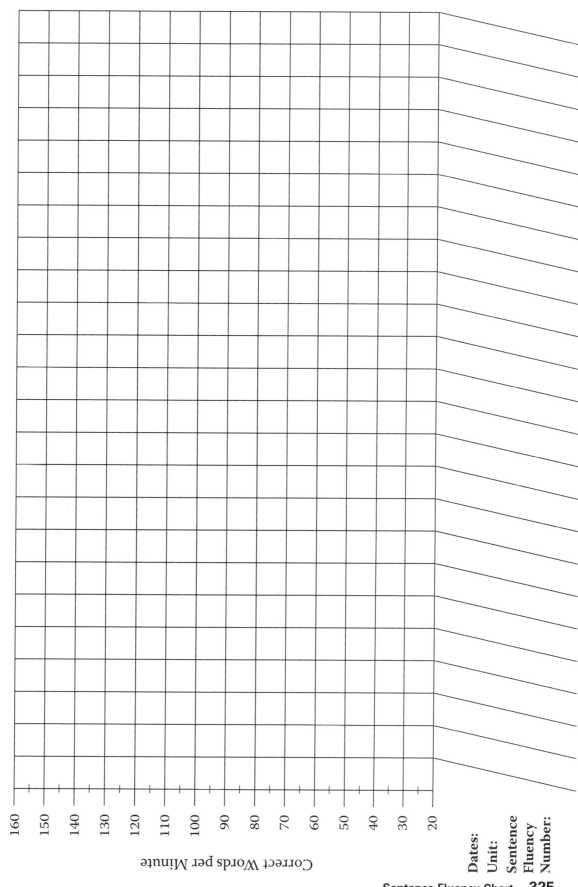

Correct Words per Minute

160 150 140 130 120 110 100 90 80 70 60 50 40 30 20

Dates:
Unit:
Sentence
Fluency
Number:

Essential Word Cards

Unit 1

are	I	is
that	the	this

Unit 2

do	said	to
who	you	your

Essential Word Cards

Unit 3

from	of	they
was	were	what

Unit 4

be	does	he
she	we	when

Essential Word Cards

Unit 5

here	there	these
those	where	why

Unit 6

down	for	her
how	me	now

Word Building Letter Cards

a	a	b	b	c	c	d
d	f	f	g	g	h	h
i	i	j	j	k	k	l
l	m	m	n	n	o	o
p	p	qu	qu	r	r	s
s	t	t	v	v	w	w
x	x	y	y	z	z	ck
ck	ll	ll	ss	ss	ff	ff
zz	zz					

Word Building Letter Cards

D	C	C	B	B	A	A
H	H	G	G	F	F	D
L	K	K	J	J	I	I
O	O	N	N	M	M	L
S	R	R	Qu	Qu	P	P
W	W	V	V	T	T	S
	Z	Z	Y	Y	X	X

Bank It

Student _____ Date_____

a	c	e

b	d	f

Student _____ Date_____

g _____

i _____

k _____

h _____

j _____

l _____

Bank It

Student _____ Date_____

m	o	qu

n	p	r

Bank It

Student _____ Date _____

s	u	x
	v	y
t	w	z